# European Economics & Law

## Competition – Single Market – Trade

*Editor*
**John Grayston**
*Partner, Eversheds*
*Brussels*

Palladian Law Publishing Ltd

© Palladian Law Publishing Ltd
Lawfully Simple Communications Ltd
1999

*Published by*
Palladian Law Publishing Ltd
Beach Road
Bembridge
Isle of Wight PO35 5NQ

www.palladianlaw.com

*in association with*
Lawfully Simple Communications Ltd
Wilmington House
High Street
East Grinstead
West Sussex RH19 3AO

ISBN 1 902558 18 9

Typeset by Heath Lodge Publishing Services
Printed in Great Britain by The Book Company Limited

# · Contents ·

# · Table of Cases & Decisions ·

# · Table of EU Treaty Articles ·

# · Table of EU Legislation ·

# · Introduction ·

I was immensely pleased when I introduced the idea for this new publication to a variety of contacts in the world of economics that they immediately grasped the idea with such enthusiasm that this work has now seen the light of day. It was initially equally pleasing when both these contributors and my publishers said that, of course, the Editor would have to provide an introductory article explaining the thinking behind the publication. As the initial, warm, positive feeling receded, I confess that it then became much harder to set down the precise reasons for proposing something which I consider to be justified simply as part of a general evolution of EU law and policy.

Economics in the EU is certainly not new. It simply cannot be said that only now in the late 1990s has economics become important. The whole EU edifice has always been justified on the basis of economic principles and then wrapped in political and legal clothing. Nevertheless, there is a sense in Brussels and among the Member States that economics is being seen to play a much more important role in justifying developments in all aspects of EU policy.

The purpose of this publication then is to react to this emerging trend. It is necessary, however, for two additional reasons. First, because economics is perceived by many to be a closed book where only economists understand the issues, answers or solutions. If such a position was ever correct it can no longer remain so because in the EU the application of the economics is left very much in the hands of non-economists. Secondly, because the economics itself is from time to time perceived to be fragile: fine for explaining the past but not so fine for predicting the future.

Moving away from such detailed considerations, there is one over-arching reason for the need for this publication: it reflects the combined disciplines that make up the EU. The EU is no more a creature of law than it is a creature of economics or indeed of policy. It is a fusion of all three elements. There are plenty of publications that look at developments in EU law, a few that look at developments in economics and very few that actually set out to look at current issues in the EU from a combined perspective of economics and law.

The subject matter for this publication is much wider than many others: *European Economics & Law* looks at competition policy, trade policy and the Single Market – not simply in order to achieve a completeness of coverage but in the belief that none of these subjects is totally self-contained. Developments in one area can have an impact or be of guidance in others, for example:

- EU and WTO trade law rules may create the ability for the EU to impose countervailing duties to counteract the impact of state subsidies, but it is the EU state aid rules which then define to what extent such subsidies can be paid to EU industry;
- whilst it was the *Silhouette* case which raised the question of compatibility of EU Single Market principles with international exhaustion, in a separate case it was the EU rules of Article 85 that were called into question when an Yves Saint Laurent dealer challenged the enforceability of a contractual clause which prevented the re-export of goods to the EU;
- in the trade law arena with the launch of the Millennium Round WTO negotiations, the whole question of whether and to what extent international trade law rules can be replaced by international competition rules looks likely to become a key issue.

By way of introduction, we can briefly look at each of these areas, starting perhaps inevitably with competition law.

## Competition law

It was the introduction of the Commission's Green Paper on Vertical Restraints which launched the current policy review that started my thought process for producing this publication. I am delighted that Luc Peeperkorn of DG IV has agreed to write on this subject for the inaugural issue.

The Green Paper seemed to me to encapsulate the feeling of change – a need to move away from rigid legal rules to more flexible (and perhaps uncertain) principles. However, looking at the Green Paper in retrospect, it merely develops themes that were evident many, many years earlier: the introduction of market share thresholds in the Technology Transfer Block Exemption (1996), the Commission's Notice on Agreements of Minor Importance (1986) and the R&D and Specialisation Block Exemptions (1985). All of these contained clear economic principles and the need for those using the measures to identify markets and calculate market shares in order to determine whether or not the provisions were applicable.

Although lawyers ritually warned clients of the dangers of relying on instruments that included a need for market share analysis, the grounds for concern were in many cases often exaggerated. First, in practical terms each of the measures contained transitional provisions; exceeding one of the limits did not immediately trigger the full application of Article 85. Moreover, as the Commission increasingly became a prisoner of its own workload, it was often difficult to identify cases where the Commission would clearly wish or be able to intervene. If the Commission – an institution allegedly steeped in economic policy and theory – would not intervene, it was even more unlikely to think that a rigorous economic approach to infringements of Article 85 would come from national courts.

It was therefore not really correct to identify the resurgence of economics as being a consequence of the Green Paper on Vertical Restraints, more it was a product of this resurgence. The growth in the importance and utility of economics probably had its origins in two other developments.

The creation of the Court of First Instance ("CFI") in 1987 was prompted by the desire to speed up the judicial process at a European level. The CFI was originally given only limited powers to deal with cases and not, for example, being able to hear Article 177 references. Nevertheless, the differences in organisation and structure of the CFI quickly led to the adoption of a growing series of cases where the CFI looked in far greater depth at the economics at issue. The readiness of the CFI to consider such issues and in a number of high profile competition cases to rule in favour of the applicant and, thus, against the Commission, not surprisingly, led to a greater readiness of the parties to such cases to argue the economics and not just the law.

The second important step, and possibly in practice the most important single step, was the introduction in 1990 of the Merger Control Regulation ("MCR"). There are many possible reasons to explain why the MCR resulted in a much heightened sense of the importance of economics in the assessment and prosecution of cases. Some of the reasons include: the short timeframe of the proceedings; the considerable risks and monies at stake; the snap-shot in time approach to the competition assessment; and perhaps also the growing ability of the parties to provide compelling evidence of markets in operation by submitting masses of computerised data on trading and purchasing patterns which a few years earlier would have been simply impossible to obtain in such a short timeframe.

Whatever the precise reason, it became clear to all parties that the basic economic market analysis of the concentration was the key to identifying an effective strategy – whether to clear or block the transaction. The next stage in the importance of the MCR was the fact that (to coin the economists' expression) there was a spill-over of the effects of the MCR approach into other areas of competition law.

If this represents the background, the question for policy-makers, economists, industrialists and lawyers alike is where does this process go from here? The resurgence of economics has not been experienced without its own particular hardships. As Holley noted when trying to identify why European economists seem to have fallen behind their American colleagues:

> "Sometimes the economist in the Community has no background in competition law, does not understand the legal issues and insists on preparing testimony on the wrong economics issues. Sometimes the economist speaks in such elevated economic terms that laymen, including most DG IV staff members, who are not economists, have little chance of understanding him ..."[1]

If this was a fair comment back in 1992, it seems surely outdated at the end of the decade. It is interesting, however, that the underlying theme of Holley's commentary is the lack of co-operation and co-ordination between the disciplines of law and economics. A significant part of the problem raised by David Holley arose because of some lawyers' uncertainty, confusion or even reluctance over when and how to bring in economists and how to share the client's brief with them. I believe that the last seven years have seen a significant change in the position. Lawyers and economists are much more aware of the contributions that they each need to make in competition cases and the dangers they risk if they do not.

## Trade law

The role of economics in trade law reveals perhaps an even more interesting background. For many years trade law was considered neither to be law (in the strict sense) or even economics, but pure policy. A decision to impose trade corrective measures against third countries

---

1 "EC competition practice: a thirty year perspective" (1992) Fordham Corporate Law Institute Annual Proceedings.

was motivated by economic policy concerns rather than justified by international trade law rules.

The broad language of the GATT seemed to support such a view. Protectionism or "Fortress Europe", as it was called at one time in the EU, was thought by many to be evidenced in the administrative implementation of EU trade policy in the 1970s and 1980s in anti-dumping proceedings or rulings on questions of the origin of goods. Defending trade cases came to be viewed as more about the procedure rather than about the substance of the case. As a result, the underlying economic analysis of the case was generally left alone.

By the 1990s this position had clearly started to change. The most significant changes have been brought about first by the revisions to the GATT in 1994 and the creation of the World Trade Organisation; and secondly by the extension of responsibility within the CFI to include a competence to deal with trade cases. It cannot really be said that these changes have as yet brought the same levels of economic rigour as are found in EU competition cases; however, the process has begun. Part of the problem remains that many of the basic principles could still benefit from further clarification.

The use of economics in cases before the CFI was not limited to competition cases. As from March 1994, the CFI's powers were extended to cover trade cases. The CFI-effect once again prevailed with more detailed judgments being handed down which looked in detail at the way in which the Commission had drawn its conclusions from the information it had obtained during the proceedings.

As the role of the European Court in such cases is one of judicial review, much of the essential case law of the Court is in fact related solely to procedural issues – to the rights of parties to challenge decisions of the Commission and subsequently on questions of procedural guarantees. However, the growing willingness of the CFI effectively to check each substantive element of the Commission's reasoning has brought a greater degree of control over the factual reasoning applied by the Commission and thus the underlying economics of its decisions.

From the practitioner's perspective, there is still a clear gap in the substantive application of economics in EU proceedings, or at the least a lack in the transparency of the economics that is applied. However, this position is evolving and there are clear signs that the Commission is struggling to develop a more economics based approach to the basic concepts of trade law. Thus, we know that in recent years the Commission has spent considerable time and sought external assistance in order to clarify the concept of injury and of Community interest in dumping and subsidy cases. Again, I am delighted that we have contributions from Peter Holmes and Cliff Stevenson who both participated in this work with the Commission.

## Single Market

Finally, we will look at the role that economics has played and continues to play in creating the Single Market. Whatever else, we can at least say that without the existence of the central economics assessment of the Cecchini Reports (1985) the whole programme would not have been given legislative priority for seven years from 1985-92. The Cecchini Reports entitled the "Non-Cost of Europe" identified barriers to trade costing the European Union ECU 200 billion. Legislative reforms were identified which, it was submitted, would achieve greater competition, change business patterns and promote innovation and ultimately reduce prices.

By the time the Commission produced its White Paper on Growth Competitiveness and Employment in 1994, problems with Europe's apparent inability to create new jobs had caused the Commission and the Member States to look again at the justification for the Single Market.

The Commission's conclusions underlined both the achievements of the Single Market programme but also the areas where further work was required. Interestingly, despite identifying that the creation of the Single Market had added about 0.5% per annum to overall EU growth, created an additional nine million jobs and produced a constant growth in levels of intra-Community trade, the Commission concluded that it was too early to tell what the actual benefits of the Single Market would be.

The White Paper recognised that however positive the effects of the Single Market, they had effectively been overtaken by greater changes in the international arena which were evidenced by the growing internationalism of commerce. Notwithstanding the success of the Single Market overall, the EU was still failing to deliver the necessary levels of growth and prosperity.

The conclusions of the White Paper thus became the post 1994 policy objectives for the European Union:

- developing the Single Market into a sustainable and business-friendly concept;

- simplifying rules where possible; and
- introducing Single Market concepts to areas which had previously been excluded from the scope of the reforms.

Bringing matters right up to date, the most tangible sign of the benefit of the Single Market is probably the fact that the Euro was introduced on 1 January 1999, launching the start of the final phase of economic and monetary union. The Euro zone of 11 Member States, whether we like it or not, defines an area within the EU where the economic benefits and realities of the Single Market have been recognised to such an extent that the political disadvantages of ceding some further element of national sovereignty to the EU have been considered to be far outweighed by the perceived political and economic benefits of further integration.

## Conclusion

Returning to the theme in the opening paragraph, in all areas of EU activity, we see the evidence of a heightened evolution and change in EU policy and its implementation.

As the Commission, the Member States and, to coin that favoured EU expression "all interested parties", seek to identify and then justify a new way forward, they are thrown back to basics that underline the whole creation: a desire to see improved economic growth and performance within the European Union.

John Grayston

# Commission's Policy · Review on Vertical · Restraints

## Lucas Peeperkorn

The author works for DG IV and has been responsible for the policy review on vertical restraints since the end of 1996. He expresses in this article his personal views only and not those of DG IV or the European Commission. He wishes to thank Donncadh Woods for allowing him to use some text from a previous joint paper.

*European Economics & Law*
Palladian Law Publishing Ltd

# Commission's Policy · Review on Vertical · Restraints

## *1.* Introduction

Distribution is a dynamic and constantly evolving sector.[1] Almost all products pass from supplier to final consumer via the distribution system which thereby performs an important function within the European Union. It accounts for almost 13% of the total Gross Domestic Product of the 15 countries of the Union, employing more than 15% of the active population and encompassing almost 30% of enterprises.[2] All industries need distribution and the level of service provided by, and efficiency of, distribution are important elements of the competitive process to reach customers. To keep distribution channels open and competitive is therefore vital for any economy.

The long-term viability of any individual member of a supply chain is becoming increasingly dependent on the ability of the entire chain to compete with the chains of other economic operators. Traditional distribution channels consisting of independent operators, each acting at arms' length and seeking to maximise their own profit rather than those of the channel as a whole are in decline. There are two major reasons for this change. First, advances in information technology have enabled more tightly managed and efficient business practices between suppliers and buyers, like just-in-time production and more customised production, that require however more co-operation. Secondly, once involved in closer vertical relations the levels of trade become mutually more dependent on each other. For example, an efficient producer would loose its competitive advantage over a less efficient rival where its distributors were inefficient and had higher operating costs than those of its competitor. Similarly, an efficient distributor would loose its

---

1 For a useful summary of changes in distribution see Chapter 1 of the Green Paper on Vertical Restraints in EC Competition Policy, COM (96) 721 final. The reader is also referred to the Green Paper on Commerce, COM (96) 530 final and to the section on distribution in the Commission's annual publication entitled "Panorama of EU Industry".
2 Annex A to the Green Paper on Commerce, COM (96) 530 final.

competitive advantage over less efficient rivals where those rivals were sourcing equivalent goods at lower prices.

It was against the background of these and other developments and a growing feeling of unease with the effectiveness of its own competition policy in the field of vertical restraints that the Commission started a thorough review of its policy in this field. The Commission commenced this review by adopting the Green Paper on Vertical Restraints in EU Competition Policy on 22 January 1997.[3]

The purpose of the Green Paper was to initiate a wide ranging consultation to assist the Commission in the formulation of future policy in this area. Numerous companies, industry and trade associations, law firms, consumer organisations and academics held discussions and organised conferences on the topic. DG IV officials, including myself, participated in a number of these discussions. The other Community institutions and Member States also formulated their opinion. Finally, the Commission received over 200 written submissions and a public hearing was held on 6 and 7 October 1997.

A number of points became clear during this consultation process:

(1) the current Block Exemptions (BEs) on exclusive distribution/ exclusive purchasing/franchising are too legalistic and form-based;

(2) that changes in the methods/formats of distribution make these BEs work more and more as a straitjacket;

(3) that the current BEs exempt clear cases of market power where vertical restraints can have serious negative effects;

(4) that for future policy a more economic approach is required, analysing vertical restraints in their market context and making the assessment dependent upon the (likely) effects on the market;

(5) that a new policy should, to the extent possible, take account of the wish for legal certainty and limitation of compliance costs.

This article treats first some of the economics of vertical restraints that will underlie a more economic approach.[4] Secondly, it sketches the

---

3 COM (96) 721 final.
4 For a useful summary of recent economic thinking on vertical restraints see Chapter 2 of the Green Paper on Vertical Restraints in EC Competition Policy. The reader is also referred to Peeperkorn "The economics of verticals", *EC Competition Policy Newsletter*, June 1998; Steiner, "How manufacturers deal with the price-cutting retailer: when are vertical restraints efficient?" (1997) *Antitrust Law Journal*, Vol 65, p 407; Dobson and Waterson "Vertical restraints and competition policy" (1996) London; Rey and Caballero-Sanz "The policy implications of the economic analysis of vertical restraints", European Commission Directorate-General for Economic and Financial Affairs Policy Paper No 119, November 1996; and "Competition policy and vertical restraints" (1994) OECD, Paris

new policy this may lead to. The article is based on the description of future policy by the Commission in its 1998 Communication on the Application of the EC Competition Rules to Vertical Restraints[5], the follow-up to the Green Paper.

## 2. **Vertical versus horizontal agreements**

It is recognised that vertical agreements are generally less harmful for competition than horizontal agreements. The main reason for treating a vertical agreement more leniently than a horizontal agreement lies in the fact that the latter may concern an agreement between competitors producing identical or substitute goods/services. In such horizontal relationships the exercise of market power by one company (higher price of its product) may benefit its competitors. This may provide an incentive to competitors to induce each other to behave anti-competitively. In vertical relationships the product of the one is the input for the other. In analogy to the withdrawn US Department of Justice Vertical Restraints Guidelines of 23 January 1985, vertical agreements are defined here as agreements or concerted practices entered into between two or more undertakings each operating at a different level of the production or distribution chain and which relate to the conditions under which undertakings may purchase, sell or resell. In as far as such an agreement restricts competition it is referred to as a vertical restraint. This means that the exercise of market power by either the upstream or downstream company would normally hurt the demand for the product of the other. The companies involved in the agreement therefore usually have an incentive to prevent the exercise of market power by the other.

However, this self-restraining character should not be over-estimated. When there is sufficiently strong inter-brand competition, the efficiency gains arising from vertical restraints are likely to be passed on to consumers and net negative effects are unlikely. However, when a company does have market power and inter-brand competition is weakened it can also use vertical restraints to try to increase its profits at the expense of its direct competitors by raising their costs and at the expense of its buyers/consumers by trying to appropriate some of their surplus. This can happen when the up-stream and down-stream company share the extra profits or when one of the two uses the vertical restraint to appropriate all the extra profits.

---

5 COM (98) 544 final.

## 3. **Negative effects of vertical agreements**

The negative effects on the market that may result from vertical restraints and that EC competition law aims at preventing are the following:

(1) foreclosure of other suppliers or other buyers by raising barriers to entry;

(2) reduction of inter-brand competition between the companies currently operating on a market, including facilitation of collusion amongst suppliers or buyers;

(3) reduction of intra-brand competition between distributors of the same brand;

(4) the creation of obstacles to market integration, including, most of all, limitations on the freedom of the consumers to purchase a good or service in any Member State they may choose.

Unlike most other competition law systems, EC competition policy has not one but two principal objectives. The first, in common with all competition enforcement authorities, is the competitive markets objective as reflected by (1), (2) and (3). The second, which is not common to other enforcement authorities, is the single market objective as reflected by (4) above. The Community has progressively broken down government erected trade barriers between Member States. It would make no sense to prohibit such state measures if they could be replaced by agreements between companies that again hinder or delay market integration.

The described negative effects may result from various vertical restraints. Agreements that are different in form may have the same substantive impact on competition. To analyse these possible negative effects it is appropriate to divide vertical restraints into four groups:

- a single branding group;
- a limited distribution group;
- a resale price maintenance group; and
- a market partitioning group.

The vertical restraints within each group have largely similar negative effects on competition. In addition tying arrangements can be discussed as a fifth category of vertical restraints. This classification is based upon what could be described as the basic elements of vertical restraints. In practice many vertical agreements contain a combination of these elements.

## Single branding group

Under the heading of single branding come those agreements that
have as their main element that the buyer is induced to concentrate his
orders for a particular type of good or service with one supplier. This
component can be found amongst others in non-compete and quantity
forcing on the buyer, where an obligation or incentive scheme agreed
between the supplier and the buyer makes the latter purchase its
requirements for a particular good or service and its substitutes only or
mainly from one supplier. There are three main effects on competition:

(1) other suppliers in that market cannot sell to the particular buyers,
    and this may lead to foreclosure of the market;

(2) it makes market shares more rigid and this may help collusion when
    applied by several suppliers; and

(3) as far as the distribution of final goods is concerned, the particular
    retailers will only sell one brand, therefore there will be no in-store
    competition in their shops.

All effects may lead to a reduction in inter-brand competition.

The reduction in inter-brand competition may be mitigated by
stronger *ex-ante* competition between suppliers to obtain the single
branding contracts, but the longer the duration the more likely it will be
that this effect will not be strong enough to compensate fully for the
lack of inter-brand competition.

## Limited distribution group

Under the heading of limited distribution come those agreements which
have as their main element that the manufacturer is selling only to one or
a limited number of buyers. This may be to restrict the number of buyers
for a particular territory or group of customers, or to select a particular
kind of buyers. This component can be found amongst others in
exclusive distribution, weaker forms of it as area of primary
responsibility and restriction on the location of an outlet, and in
exclusive customer allocation. The supplier limits its sales to only one
buyer for a certain territory or class of customers. It is also found in
exclusive supply and quantity forcing on the supplier, where an
obligation or incentive scheme agreed between the supplier and the
buyer makes the former sell only or mainly to one buyer. Also selective
distribution contains this element as the conditions imposed on or

agreed with the selected dealers usually limit their number. After-market sales restrictions contain the same element by limiting the original supplier's sales possibilities. There are three main effects on competition:

(1) certain buyers within that market can no longer buy from this particular supplier, and this may lead, in particular in the case of exclusive supply, to foreclosure of the purchase market;

(2) when most or all of the competing suppliers limit the number of retailers, this may facilitate collusion either at the distributor or supplier level; and

(3) as far as the distribution of final goods is concerned, since fewer distributors will offer this good it will also lead to a reduction of intra-brand competition.

In the case of wide exclusive territories or exclusive customer allocation the result may be total elimination of intra-brand competition. This reduction of intra-brand competition can in turn lead to a weakening of inter-brand competition.

## Resale price maintenance group

Under the heading of resale price maintenance come those agreements which have as their main element that the buyer is obliged or induced to resell not below a certain price, at a certain price or not above a certain price. This group comprises minimum, fixed, maximum and recommended resale prices. Maximum and recommended resale prices, while as such not having negative effects, may work as fixed RPM. As RPM relates to the resale price it is mainly relevant for the distribution of final goods. There are two main effects of minimum and fixed RPM on competition:

(1) the distributors can no longer compete on price for that brand, leading to a total elimination of intra-brand price competition; and

(2) there is increased transparency on price and responsibility for price changes, making horizontal collusion between manufacturers or distributors easier, at least in concentrated markets.

The reduction in intra-brand competition may, as it leads to less downward pressure on the price for the particular good, have as an indirect effect a reduction of inter-brand competition.

## Market partitioning group

Under the heading of market partitioning come agreements which have as their main element that the buyer is restricted in where it either sources or resells a particular good or service. This component can be found in exclusive purchasing, where an obligation or incentive scheme agreed between the supplier and the buyer makes the latter purchase its requirements for a particular good or service exclusively from the designated supplier, but leaving the buyer free to buy and sell competing goods or services. It also includes territorial resale restrictions, customer resale restrictions and prohibitions of resale.

The main effect on competition is a reduction of intra-brand competition that may help the supplier to partition the market and thus hinder market integration. This may facilitate price discrimination. When most or all of the competing suppliers limit the sourcing or resale possibilities of their buyer, this may facilitate collusion, either at the distributor or supplier level.

## Tying arrangements

The main element of tying is the requirement that the buyer of a good or service purchases a second distinct good or service as a condition of purchasing the first. The first good or service is referred to as the "tying" good or service and the second is referred to as the "tied" good or service.

Its main effect on competition is that the buyer may pay a higher price for the tied product than it would otherwise do and it may also lead to foreclosure of the market of the tied product and reduce inter-brand competition in that market.

# 4. Positive effects of vertical agreements

It is important to recognise that vertical agreements often have positive effects. When a company has no market power it can only try to increase its profits by optimising its manufacturing or distribution processes. In a number of situations vertical restraints may be helpful in this respect as the usual arm's length dealings between supplier and buyer, determining only price and quantity of a certain transaction, can lead to a sub-optimal level of investments and sales.

The following general observations can be made about the likely positive effects of vertical restraints:[6]

(1)  The first and main reason a sub-optimal level of investments and sales may result is the existence of some form of free rider problem. The person who makes an effort may not be able to appropriate all the benefits his or her effort engenders and may therefore be inclined to invest sub-optimally. This may be the result of free riding by one buyer on the promotion efforts of another buyer. This type of problem is most common at the wholesale and retail level, but not at the level of intermediate goods or services. Exclusive distribution or similar restrictions may be helpful in avoiding such free riding. Free riding can also occur between suppliers, for example, where one supplier invests in promotion at the buyer's premises, in general at the retail level, that may also attract customers for its competitors. Non-compete type restraints can help to overcome this type of free riding.

For there to be a problem there needs to be a real free rider issue. Free riding between distributors can only occur on pre-sales services and not on after-sales services. The good will usually need to be relatively new or technically complex as the customer otherwise may very well know what he wants from past purchases. And the good must be of a reasonably high value as otherwise it is not attractive for a customer to go to one shop for information and to another to buy. Lastly, it must not be practical for the supplier to impose by contract on all distributors effective service requirements concerning the pre-sales services.

Free riding between suppliers is also restricted to specific situations. A non-compete type agreement may help capture the full benefits in case the promotion takes place in the retail outlets and is not brand specific.

(2)  A special case of free riding may be linked to opening up or entering new markets. In case a manufacturer wants to enter a new geographic market, for example by exporting for the first time to another country, this may involve special "first time investments" to establish the brand in the market. In order to convince a local

---

6  While trying to give a fair overview of the various justifications for vertical restraints, this list does not claim to be complete.

distributor to make these investments it may be necessary to provide territorial protection to the distributor so that it can recoup these investments by charging temporarily a higher price. Distributors based in other markets should then be refrained for a limited period from trying to sell in the new market. This is a special case of the free rider problem described under (1).

(3)  A case of longer duration of free riding between different markets could exist when the manufacturer has a different promotional strategy in the different markets. For example, assume a manufacturer does most brand promotion itself in its home market while it leaves the promotion to be done by its (exclusive) distributor(s) in other markets. It may have good reasons of economies of scale or market expertise for this. The manufacturer's promotion costs will be part of its ex-factory price in the home market while it can and may have to apply, under competitive conditions, a lower ex-factory price in the other markets. The manufacturer may want to restrain to some extent its distributors in the latter markets from re-importing the product into its home market to prevent free riding on the promotional efforts of the manufacturer paid by the retailers in the home market through a higher ex-factory price.

(4)  A special form of free riding is the certification free rider issue. The hypothesis is that certain retailers perform a valuable service by identifying "good" products. The fact that these retailers sell a certain product signifies to the consumer that it is a good buy. In such cases selling through these retailers may be vital for the introduction of new products. If the manufacturer can not initially limit its sales to the premium stores, it runs the risk of being de-listed and the product introduction may fail. The manufacturer may use a restriction of the exclusive distribution or selective distribution kind, possibly long enough to guarantee introduction, but not so long as to hinder large scale dissemination.

(5)  Another special form of free riding is the so-called "hold-up" problem. Sometimes there are specific investments to be made by either the supplier or the buyer, such as in special equipment or training. For example, a component manufacturer that has to build/buy new machines and tools in order to satisfy a particular requirement of one of its customers. The investor may not commit the necessary investments before particular supply arrangements are fixed.

However, as in the other free riding examples, there are a number of conditions that have to be met before the risk of under-investment is real or significant. First, the investment must be sunk and specific to deal with that other party only. An investment is considered sunk when, upon exiting the market or after termination of the contract, the investment can not be sold unless at a significant loss. An investment is specific if it can only be used to produce that particular component, to store that particular brand etc and thus can not be used profitably to produce or resell alternatives. Secondly, it must be a long-term investment that is not recouped in the short run. Thirdly, the investment must be asymmetric, *i.e.* one party to the contract invests more than the other party. When these conditions are met there is usually a good reason to have a vertical restraint for the duration it takes to depreciate the investment. The adequate vertical restraint will be of the non-compete type or quantity forcing type when the investment is made by the supplier and of the exclusive distribution, exclusive customer allocation or exclusive supply type when the investment is made by the buyer.

(6) A similar hold-up problem may arise when the investment is not specific but the investment is made at the premises of the other party to the contract. The more the investments are sunk the more costly it becomes to take the investments back and the more it is necessary for the investor to sell the investment to the other party when the contract is terminated. However, this may give rise to transaction costs. If these costs are significant this may require a vertical restraint with a limited duration; of the non-compete type or quantity forcing type when the investment is made by the supplier and of the exclusive distribution or exclusive supply type when the investment is made by the buyer.

(7) Another special form of the hold-up problem may arise in case of transfer of substantial know-how, either by the buyer to the supplier or the other way around. The know-how, once provided, can not be taken back and the provider of the know-how may not want it to be used for or by its competitors. In as far as the know-how was not readily available to the receiver, is substantial and is necessary for the operation of the vertical agreement such transfer may form a good reason to agree an exclusive relationship. In case the know-how is provided by the supplier this may justify a non-compete type of restriction. In case the know-how is provided by

the buyer this may justify an exclusive supply type of restriction. In case there is a continuing transfer of know-how or a continuing risk of losing know-how to competitors a restriction protecting the know-how may be necessary for the duration of the agreement.

(8) Another sub-optimal outcome that can be remedied by using a vertical restraint may occur when there are economies of scale in distribution. In order to have these economies exploited and thereby see a lower retail price for its product the manufacturer may want to concentrate the resale of its product with a limited number of distributors. For this it could use exclusive distribution, quantity forcing in the form of a minimum purchasing requirement, selective distribution containing such a requirement or exclusive purchasing. Such scale economies may be particularly potent at the wholesale level.

(9) Another reason to engage in a vertical restraint with a limited duration may be sub-optimal investment by either buyer or supplier as a result of capital market imperfections. The usual providers of capital (banks, equity markets) may provide capital sub-optimally especially when they have imperfect information on the quality of the borrower or there is an inadequate basis to secure the loan. The buyer or supplier may have better information and be able, through an exclusive relationship, to obtain extra security for its investment. In case the supplier provides the loan to the buyer this may lead to non-compete or quantity forcing on the buyer. In case the buyer provides the loan to the supplier this may be the reason for having exclusive supply or quantity forcing on the supplier.

(10) Another way in which a vertical restraint may increase sales is by imposing a certain measure of uniformity and quality standardisation on the distributors to help create a brand image and attractiveness to the final consumers. This can for example be found in selective distribution and franchising.

(11) A last, rather hypothetical reason to engage in a vertical restraint is the possibility of "double marginalisation". In case both the manufacturer and the distributor have market power each will set its price above marginal cost. They both add their margin that exceeds the one that would exist under competition. This may result in a retail price that even exceeds the monopoly price an

integrated company would charge, to the detriment of their collective profits and consumers. In this case quantity forcing on the buyer or maximum RPM could help the manufacturer bring the price down to monopoly level.

The above 11 situations make clear that under certain conditions vertical agreements are likely to help realise efficiencies and enter new markets which may offset possible negative effects. The case is in general strongest for vertical restraints of a limited duration which help the introduction of new complex products or protect specific investments.

## 5. **The Communication of the Commission**

### Introduction

On 30 September 1998 the Commission adopted its Communication on the Application of the EC Competition Rules to Vertical Restraints. This policy paper sets out the Commission's proposal for a new policy in the field of vertical restraints. This proposal is based on the thesis that in the absence of market power, a presumption of legality for vertical restraints can be made except for certain hardcore restrictions. It is proposed that the Commission will adopt a wide block exemption Regulation complemented by guidelines. It is important to recognise that the Communication sets out a general framework and that a number of issues have been left open at this stage. Many of the precise details of the new policy will only be decided after the consultation process that will precede the adoption of the new block exemption Regulation and guidelines.

Before the Commission can adopt the new block exemption Regulation the Commission will have to obtain new legislative powers from the Council. Therefore, in addition to the Communication, the Commission also adopted two proposals for Council Regulations amending, respectively, Council Regulation 19/65/EEC of 2 March 1965, with a view to granting the Commission the necessary legislative powers to implement the proposed new policy, and Council Regulation 17 of 6 February 1962, with a view to extending the waiver from notification provided for in Article 4(2) to all vertical agreements. The Council's working group started to examine these proposals on 4 November 1998 and discussions are expected to be concluded in the first half of 1999 under the German presidency. It is envisaged that new competition rules for the distribution of goods and services should be in place for the year 2000.

## Outline of the policy proposal

In its Communication, the Commission recommends a shift from the current policy relying on form-based requirements with sector specific rules to an economic effects based system covering virtually all sectors of distribution.[7] It is proposed that this be achieved by one, very wide, block exemption Regulation that covers all vertical restraints concerning intermediate and final goods and services except for a limited number of hardcore restraints for which individual exemption is also unlikely. It is based mainly on a black clause approach, *i.e.* defining what is not block exempted instead of defining what is exempted. This form of deregulation removes the strait-jacket effect, a structural flaw inherent in any system which attempts to identify clauses which are exempted.

The principal objective of such a wide and flexible block exemption is to grant companies who lack market power, and most companies lack market power, a safe harbour within which it is no longer necessary for them to assess the validity of their agreements under the EC competition rules. In order to preserve competition and to limit the extent of this exemption to companies which do not have significant market power, the block exemption would establish one or two market share thresholds, beyond which companies could not avail themselves of the safe harbour.

For companies with market shares above the threshold(s) of the block exemption it must be stressed that there would be no presumption of illegality. The market share threshold would only serve to distinguish those agreements which are presumed to be legal from those that may require individual examination. To assist companies in carrying out such an examination the Commission intends to issue a set of guidelines covering basically three issues: the scope of application of Article 85(1) above the market share cap(s), the Commission's policy under Article 85(3) and its policy of withdrawal of the benefit of the block exemption, particularly in cumulative effect cases. Any such

---

7 The block exemption Regulation on car distribution, which expires in 2002, is not covered by the current proposal.

guidelines should set out clear rules so as to allow companies to make in most cases their own assessment under Article 85(1) and (3). The objective must be to reduce the enforcement cost for industry and to eliminate as far as possible notifications of agreements that do not raise any serious competition problem. This objective is also furthered by the foreseen change of Regulation 17. At the moment, an agreement falling within Article 85(1) is automatically null and void where it is not notified. This leads to an increased number of notifications. By applying Article 4(2) of Regulation 17 to vertical agreements, these agreements will no longer be null and void just because they are not notified while the Commission can give a retroactive exemption in case the agreement is notified at a later date.

The Communication leaves open the choice between a system based on one or two thresholds, however the odds seem better for a one threshold system. In a one–threshold system all vertical restraints and their combinations, with the exception of hardcore restraints, are automatically exempted up to the level of a single market share. The level of such a cap is likely to be in the range 25-35%. The advantage of a single threshold system arises from its simplicity, there being no necessity to define specific vertical restraints other than hardcore. Only in case conditions are being attached to the coverage by the BE of certain vertical restraints, like a duration limit for non-compete obligations, this requires additional definition of these particular vertical restraints. Such a system would take better account of the requirements of legal certainty and limitation of compliance costs.

In a two–threshold system the first and main market share cap would be 20%. Below this it is assumed that vertical restraints have no significant net negative effects and therefore all vertical restraints and their combinations, with the exception of the hardcore restraints, are exempted. Above the 20% threshold there is room to exempt certain vertical restraints up to a higher level of 40%. This second threshold would cover vertical restraints that, on the basis of economic thinking or past policy experience, lead to less serious restrictions of competition (*e.g.* exclusive distribution, exclusive purchasing, non-exclusive type of arrangements, such as quantity forcing on the buyer or supplier, agreements between SMEs). A two–threshold system has the advantage that it can provide for an economically justified graduation in the treatment of vertical restraints that does justice to differences in likely anti-competitive effects. The principle drawback of such a system is its complexity given that one has to identify and define the individual vertical restraints covered by the higher threshold. While every effort would be made to define these vertical restraints in terms of their effect rather than form, it would not be possible totally to avoid formalistic definitions given the need for legal security. For example, under a two–threshold system it is necessary to distinguish between quantity forcing (covered up to the higher threshold) and non-compete (covered up to lower threshold). While it is clear that an obligation on a buyer to purchase only one brand in a particular product market amounts to non-compete and that an obligation on a buyer to reserve 40% of its purchases in a particular product market for only one brand amounts to quantity forcing, the dividing line between the two is not easy to define. Therefore, under a two–threshold system there will remain a certain element of unwanted form shopping.

The choice has been made to propose one wide block exemption Regulation instead of different Regulations for specific forms of vertical restraints. It thus treats different forms of vertical restraints having similar effects in a similar way; preventing unjustified differentiation between forms. In this way it is avoided, to the greatest extent possible, to have a policy bias in the choice companies make concerning their formats of distribution. The company's choice should be based on commercial merit and not, as under the current system, on unjustified differences in exemptability. For similar reasons of coherence and unity of policy it is proposed not to retain sector specific rules for beer and petrol. There are no sufficient economic or legal reasons to continue to have a special regime for these sectors. In as far as sector specific treatment is justified this should be addressed in guidelines.

The general rule will be that the benefit of the BE will be dependent upon the individual supplier's market share. Only in case of exclusive supply, that is when the supplier is obliged to sell to one buyer only, is the market share of the buyer decisive for the benefit of the BE.

In the Communication the following are defined as hardcore restrictions that always fall outside the outlined block exemption:

(1) fixed resale prices or minimum resale prices;

(2) maximum resale prices or recommended resale prices which in reality amount to fixed or minimum resale prices as a result of a pressure exercised by any of the parties; and

(3) absolute territorial protection.

In addition, the Commission proposes in the Communication a number of other possible hardcore restrictions. As these may have been revised already by the time of publication of this article they are not further mentioned here.[8]

Negative effects on competition arising from the cumulative effect of networks of different suppliers, where the network of each individual supplier assessed in isolation benefits from the block exemption Regulation, will be dealt with by withdrawal of the block exemption Regulation with effect for the future. This is because in general only a competition authority can be expected to carry out the sector–wide investigations required to justify intervention in cases of cumulative effect. It is proposed that not only the Commission but also national authorities will have the powers to withdraw the benefit of the block exemption with effect for the future.

An additional mechanism is proposed for the treatment of cumulative effects in selective distribution. The Commission will have the power to declare the block exemption inapplicable for the future in a particular market where more than two-thirds of total sales is channelled through parallel networks of selective distribution. Such a Regulation will have to be published in the *Official Journal* and will only enter into force following the expiry of a transitional period of not less than six months.

It is proposed that the block exemption Regulation will cover associations of independent retailers that associate themselves to collectively purchase goods for resale to final customers under a common format. To benefit from the block exemption, the individual members of the association must be SMEs. It is recognised that there are horizontal aspects to these associations, therefore the benefit of the block exemption is also subject to the proviso that the horizontal aspects do not violate Article 85.

It is proposed to incorporate in the block exemption Regulation duration limits on non-compete agreements in view of their potential foreclosure effects. Consideration is being given to also incorporate a duration limit for exclusive purchase agreements when combined with quantity forcing. Consideration is also being given to dispensing with duration limits for non-compete obligations imposed by the supplier, where the supplier owns the premises from which the buyer operates. The guidelines will take account of the need for longer duration limits where justified by long term investments.

---

8  See Section V.3 of the Communication.

Finally, the block exemption will have transitional provisions to provide for the adaptation of contracts covered by the current BEs and in existence on the date of entry into force of the Regulation.

## 6. **Conclusion**

The Communication proposes a radical overhaul of competition policy towards distribution agreements. The objective is to shift towards a more economic approach while increasing the overall level of legal security for companies by providing them with a safe harbour. Within such a safe harbour, delineated by a market share threshold, it would no longer be necessary for companies to assess the validity of their agreements under the EC competition rules. Outside the safe harbour guidelines will assist companies in the assessment of their vertical agreements under Article 85.

It is submitted that implementation of the policy set out in the Communication will, to a large extent, restore freedom of contract to economic operators. Instead of having to fit their agreements into formalistic block exemptions they will, where they lack market power, be free to adopt distribution formats which correspond with commercial reality and the demands of their customer base. However, this freedom will of necessity exclude hardcore restrictions. Care will have to be taken when entering into distribution arrangements not to incorporate a clause or operate a practice which gives rise to a hardcore restraint. The scope of this limitation on the freedom of action of economic operators will not become fully apparent until the hardcore restrictions have been clearly defined in the block exemption Regulation.

Finally, given that the new policy is based on market power and not formalistic clauses it should allow the Commission to concentrate on major cases of hard-core, oligopolistic markets with collusive tendencies, foreclosure etc so as to show more teeth when necessary to better protect competition and consumer welfare.

Lucas Peeperkorn

# Oscar Bronner
# · Legitimate Refusals ·
# to Supply

## Simon Bishop and Derek Ridyard

The authors are economists with the London office of NERA's (National Economic Research Associates) European Competition Team and advise clients involved in investigations both before the European Commission and national authorities. National Economic Research Associates, 15 Stratford Place, London W1N 9AF. Telephone (44-171) 629 6787: Fax (44-171) 495 3216.

*European Economics & Law*
Palladian Law Publishing Ltd

# Oscar Bronner
# · Legitimate Refusals ·
# to Supply

On 26 November 1998, the European Court of Justice (ECJ) delivered its judgment on the Oscar Bronner case.[1] This case was referred to the ECJ by the Oberlandesgericht Wien and concerned a national dispute between two Austrian daily newspaper suppliers. The ECJ was asked to consider whether the refusal of Mediaprint, a publisher of daily newspapers, to grant access to Bronner, publisher of the daily newspaper *Der Standard*, to its national home delivery service constituted an abuse of a dominant position.

Bronner claimed that Mediaprint's market share of 45% was evidence of a dominant position. Since the sales of Bronner's *Der Standard* were too small to justify an investment in its own home delivery service, and since the alternatives open to it – postal delivery, or sale of *Der Standard* through conventional newspaper retail outlets, for example – were inferior, Bronner claimed that Mediaprint's national home delivery service constituted an essential facility. Refusal to grant access therefore, in its view, constituted an abuse of a dominant position under Article 86 of the EC Treaty.

In an important step in EC competition law, the Court rejected this complaint and, in so doing, provided a welcome antidote to the creeping over-use of the essential facilities doctrine. This article examines the reasoning of both the Advocate General[2] and the Court. This reasoning, whilst not providing definitive guidance, begins to challenge some of the economic ambiguities that arise in the application of the essential facilities doctrine.

---

1 Case C-7/97 *Oscar Bronner* v *Mediaprint*, judgment of the Court (Sixth Chamber), 26 November 1998.
2 Opinion of Advocate General Jacobs on Case C-7/98, delivered on 28 May 1998.

# 1. **Problems with the essential facilities doctrine**

The term "essential facility" was first used by the EC Commission in two related Article 86 cases involving Sealink during the early 1990s. The Commission defined an essential facility as follows:

> "a facility or infrastructure without access to which competitors cannot provide services to their customers."[3]

The problems with applying the essential facilities doctrine can be seen immediately from the ambiguities in this definition. For example:

- Must it be *physically impossible* for competitors to replicate the facility through their own endeavours irrespective of the cost? If so, few assets would meet the criterion unless there were some outright legal prohibition on doing so, for example, if the facility owner were a state-owned utility operating under a monopoly charter.
- Alternatively, must it simply be *commercially unattractive* for competitors to replicate the facility? If so, the criterion seems to encompass cases in which the plaintiff firm demands access to the dominant firm's facility for no better reason than that the dominant firm is more efficient than the plaintiff.

The former interpretation would virtually confine essential facilities to cases where state-controlled utility industries enjoyed a legal monopoly, and would preclude the use of the essential facilities doctrine in cases where market forces generate genuine bottleneck monopoly problems.

The latter interpretation risks an essential facility being defined as an asset which it would be *inconvenient* for competitors to have to replicate. The doctrine could then be applied for no better reason than that the dominant firm was more efficient than the plaintiff. Competition law intervention would then be used as a low-cost alternative to the arduous and time-consuming process of *competing* to make better products than one's rivals.

It is critical for the application of this principle that one is able to discriminate between a refusal to grant access that merely involves the lawful exercise of property rights and refusal to grant access that harms

---

3 *B & I Line plc* v *Sealink Harbours and Sealink Stena*, Commission Decision 1992, and *Sea Containers* v *Sealink*, Commission Decision 1993. The main distinction between the two cases is that *B & I Line* (Irish Ferries) was already operating out of Holyhead, whereas Sea Containers invoked essential facilities arguments in an attempt to gain access to Holyhead to operate a new service.

competition. This need is recognised by both the Advocate General and the Court.

## 2. **Competition not competitors**

The Opinion of the Advocate General offers the useful clarification that the primary purpose of Article 86 is to prevent the distortion of competition, and in particular to safeguard the interests of consumers rather than to protect the position of particular competitors.[4]

This important principle underpins the ECJ's reasoning. In assessing whether a national daily distribution system constituted an essential facility, the Court noted that there are alternatives to home delivery. Hence, the denial of access to Mediaprint's system, "even though [the alternatives] may be less advantageous", does not threaten the continued operation of the plaintiff's business. Here, the judgment picks up on a theme outlined in the Advocate General's Opinion, which states:

> "the mere fact that by retaining a facility for its own use a dominant undertaking retains an advantage over a competitor cannot justify requiring access to it."[5]

Moreover, the ECJ's judgment also draws a distinction between what is essential for competition and what is essential for individual competitors. Again, this aspect of the judgment echoes the Advocate General's sceptical comments:

> "in order for refusal of access to amount to an abuse, it must be extremely difficult not merely for the undertaking demanding access but for any other undertaking to compete."[6]

It is not therefore material that a newspaper with a low circulation would not find it economic to establish a nation-wide distribution system. Rather, in applying the essential facilities doctrine, one must establish that the level of investment required to set up an alternative nation-wide home distribution system would be such as to deter an efficient publisher who was convinced that the market could sustain a competing system.

---

4 Advocate General's Opinion, para 58.
5 *Ibid*, para 57.
6 *Ibid*, para 65.

## 3. **Blunting competition**

In general, it is easy to find situations in which compulsory access might lead to an increase in competition. But such competitive gains are likely to be short-lived since compulsory access will undermine dynamic incentives which are of equal if not more importance to economic efficiency than static considerations. As the Advocate General noted, in the long term it is generally pro-competitive and in the interest of consumers to allow a company to retain for its own use facilities which it has developed for the purpose of its business.

> "For example, if access to a production, purchasing or distribution facility were allowed too easily there would be no incentive for a competitor to develop competing facilities. Thus while competition was increased in the short term it would be reduced in the long term. Moreover the incentive for a dominant undertaking to invest in efficient facilities would be reduced if its competitors were, upon request, able to share the benefits."[7]

Just in case the severity of this warning was missed by the reader, the Advocate General goes on to state:

> "To accept Bronner's contention would be to lead the Community and national authorities and courts into detailed regulation of the Community markets, entailing the fixing of prices and conditions of supply in large sectors of the economy. Intervention on that scale would not only be unworkable but would also be anti-competitive in the longer term and indeed would scarcely be compatible with a free economy."[8]

In other words, the imposition of compulsory access is a last resort, to be applied only when all hope of normal competition has been abandoned.

## 4. **Access implies detailed price regulation**

This last point leads to a third key issue raised by essential facilities, namely recognition that compulsory access necessarily involves detailed price regulation. Herein lies a key distinction between the Advocate General's and the Commission's attitude towards essential facilities. In Sealink and other cases, when it comes to the thorny question of access terms the Commission has relied on assertions that access prices should

---

7 *Ibid*, para 57.
8 *Ibid*, para 69.

be "fair and non-discriminatory". This gives the impression that detailed regulation of access pricing, if it is a problem at all, belongs to someone else.[9] In contrast, the Advocate General and implicitly also the Court realise that application of the essential facilities doctrine brings with it some uncomfortable responsibilities.

## 5. **Conclusion**

Whilst the Court has not provided certainty, and, perhaps regrettably, has not been as explicit in setting out the rationale for its judgment as the Advocate General's Opinion, it has stated a strong case for a more measured use of the Article 86 powers in this area, recognising that a decision to subvert the normal workings of a competitive market by requiring firms to assist their competitors should not be taken lightly. In real world markets in which competition is a dynamic process, the use of competition law to level the playing field between winners and losers can do serious harm to the competitive process and to consumer interests. The Court's judgment in *Oscar Bronner* provides a significant step in defining the limiting principles that properly apply to the essential facilities doctrine.

## 6. **Postscript on the Sealink cases**

The final word on this discussion belongs to the 1993 *Sea Containers v Sealink* Article 86 case. In particular, it is worth reviewing how competition in the market for passenger ferry services between Britain and Ireland on the central corridor routes has evolved since that decision was taken.

In its decisions, the Commission deemed Holyhead port in North Wales to be an essential facility. Sealink, the owner of Holyhead port and also the main ferry operator on the route from Holyhead to Dun Laoghaire near Dublin, was therefore required by the 1993 Commission Decision to make the port available to Sea Containers, a rival ferry operator. But Sea Containers[10] never took up this option to operate from

---

9  For a discussion of some of the cases, see Ridyard, "Essential facilities and the obligation to supply competitors under UK and EC competition law" (1996) ECLR, Vol 17, Issue 8.

10 One explanatory factor appears to have been the launch by Sealink of its own fast cat service on this route, which reduced the attractiveness to Sea Containers of its proposed Holyhead-Dublin service.

Holyhead. Instead, since 1996, it has been operating a passenger service on the central corridor from the port of Liverpool rather than Holyhead, and as from 1998 it has installed a fast catamaran vessel on the route of a similar size to the one it had originally planned to operate on between Holyhead and Dublin in 1993.

At the time of the complaint, the Commission had dismissed the possibility that services operating from Liverpool (which was not at that time being used for passenger ferry services to Ireland) could be effective substitutes for those operating form Holyhead:

> "the Dublin to Liverpool journey [is] so much longer that the Liverpool port is not substitutable for Holyhead for the purpose of passenger and car ferry services."[11]

It is true that the sea crossing from Liverpool is longer, taking a little over two hours more than the Holyhead route. On the other hand, the Holyhead passenger faces a drive across North Wales of some 80 miles (approximately 130 km) after leaving the main motorway, whereas Liverpool docks are well served by two major motorway routes. Consumers therefore face a trade-off between sea crossing time, car journey time, fuel costs and convenience – a trade-off not adequately assessed by the Commission. As Sea Containers' own brochure puts it:

> "Why put up with the stress and fuel costs of driving an extra 2 hours from Liverpool when you can sail direct from Liverpool, so easily reached by the motorway network?"

Thus, a retrospective look at the *Sea Containers* case provides salient illustrations of the dangers of misuse of the essential facilities doctrine.

## Claims that assets are essential are overstated

Whilst Holyhead might be the most attractive port for central corridor passenger traffic, this interesting real life experiment has revealed that it is not, after all, the only possibility. By Sea Containers' actions, we see that Holyhead is at most a facility without access to which competitors would find it *inconvenient* to provide a service to customers. The Commission's own stated test of an *essential* facility has been shown not to apply, and nor does Holyhead port satisfy the Court's test from the *Oscar Bronner* case.

---

11 1993 Commission Decision, para 63.

**Granting access can blunt competition and reduce choice**

The launch of the Sea Containers service from Liverpool represents the kind of innovation and customer choice extension that would, paradoxically, have been stifled had the Commission's intended intervention been successful. Out of the *inconvenience* to Sea Containers in not gaining access to Sealinks assets at Holyhead port has come a new, innovative service offering to the traveller. Here, in the very market that gave birth to the essential facility concept in Europe, we see a tangible illustration of the kind of product quality suppression and damage to dynamic incentives that critics of the essential facilities doctrine fear from intervention under the essential facilities doctrine.

Simon Bishop
Derek Ridyard

# Boundaries of the Firm in EC Competition Law

## Sarah Beeston and Tom Hoehn

Sarah Beeston is head of the European and competition law team of PricewaterhouseCoopers in the Netherlands; Marten Meesweg 25, 3009 AV Rotterdam; Sarah.Beeston@nl.pwcglobal.com

Tom Hoehn is Managing Director of LECG Ltd, Brussels Office and Visiting Fellow, Management School, Imperial College, London; Tom.Hoehn@lecg.com.

*European Economics & Law*

Palladian Law Publishing Ltd

# Boundaries of the Firm in EC Competition Law

## 1. Introduction

Anti-trust analysis is concerned with:

(1) firms that exert market power through unilateral actions;

(2) mergers between firms that create or enhance market power; and

(3) firms that either explicitly or implicitly co-ordinate their behaviour and thereby distort, prevent or reduce competition in a market.

Consideration of these three possible scenarios requires the prior identification of the following two essential elements:

- the relevant market; and
- the relevant economic entities.

Competition issues need to be assessed in the context of the market in which the firms concerned are active. This has consistently been recognised in the application of Article 86 of the EC Treaty and the EC Merger Regulation.[1] In the context of merger proceedings, in particular, much time is spent on the correct definition of the relevant market, using economic analysis enhanced by a number of quantitative tests.[2] Market definition also plays an important, if somewhat less recognised, role in the consideration of possible distortions of competition in the application of Article 85 of the EC Treaty. Its role in this context is likely to increase as a result of the greater significance given to market share criteria in relation to the determination of agreements of minor importance[3] and the proposal to increase the role of market shares in the application of Article 85 and block exemptions.[4] In this context,

---

1  Reg 4064/89 of 21 December 1989 on the control of concentrations between undertakings, OJ 1990 L257/14 (the "Merger Regulation"); Commission Notice on the Definition of the Relevant Market for the Purposes of Community Competition Law, OJ 1997 C372.

2  See, for example, *Proctor & Gamble/BP Schickedanz*, Case No IV/M.430, EMCR 1511.

3  Notice on Agreements of Minor Importance, OJ 1997 C372/13.

4  Commission Communication on Vertical Restraints (98/C, 365/03) OJ 1998 C365/3.

and recognising the importance of market definition, the Commission has drawn up a Notice on the definition of the relevant market.[5]

By contrast, the definition of the relevant economic entity (*i.e.* the firm) for competition analysis has been given much less attention. While competition lawyers will often consult economists on the correct market definition, they will rarely consider the need for economic advice as to the correct delimitation of the firm although the two steps, market definition and identification of the firm, are clearly related. The calculation of market shares, an important indication of market power, requires the determination of the boundaries of the firm, as well as the size of the market. Overestimating the size of a firm can lead to market share figures that are too high. This may have significant implications for the assessment of market power under Article 86 or the Merger Regulation. It is also important for the application of Article 85 to decide whether an agreement is between more than one party and may therefore restrict competition or whether it is merely a form of regulation of the internal affairs of a single undertaking which falls outside Article 85.

Figures 1 and 2 (p 30) illustrate the importance of the correct identification of the relevant economic entity in EC competition law considering both horizontal ownership links and vertical links.

In Figure 1 Manufacturers A, B, C, D and E produce widgets. Manufacturers A and B each supply a significant part (respectively 20% and 25%) of the market. A owns 25% of B. What is the relevant economic entity for the purpose of applying EC competition law? Is it the combined operations of A and B, or do these two entities need to be treated separately? In the first case Article 86 may apply to the actions of A and B and any acquisition by A or B will be assessed under the Merger Regulation on the basis of the combined market position of A and B as increased by the target company; in the latter case Article 85(1) may be relevant to agreements between A and B.

The identification of the relevant economic entity is also relevant in EC law in the following circumstances:

- when enumerating the parties to an agreement for the purposes of the application of a block exemption;[6]

---

5 OJ 1997 C372/5.
6 Case 170/83 *Hydrotherm Geratebau* v *Compact* [1984] ECR 299. In this case, Reg 67/67 on the application of Article 85 of the Treaty to categories of exclusive dealing agreements was held to apply in a situation where several legally independent entities were acting as one contracting party provided that those undertakings constituted an economic unit for the purpose of the agreement.

Horizontal ownership links
E
20%
A
20%
D
18%
B
25%
C
17%

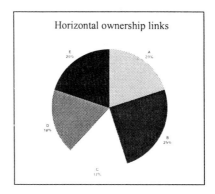

*Figure 1*

Figure 2 illustrates a distributor-retailer relationship. Agreements between upstream distributors and their retailer customers may fall within Article 85(1) if the retailers are considered independent. If they are integrated, this will not be the case. The distributors will be considered to be active in the retail market and their market position will be assessed on the retail, as well as the upstream, level. This may have implications for the application of Article 86 to the activities of distributors with strong retailer customers and in the assessment of a merger between distributors.

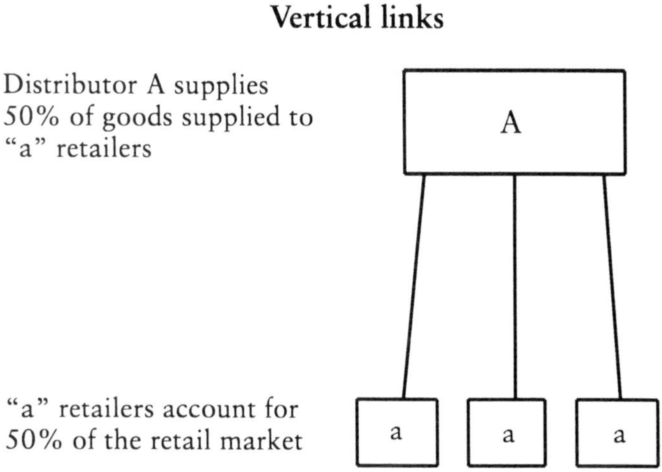

Vertical links
Distributor A supplies 50% of goods supplied to "a" retailers
A
"a" retailers account for 50% of the retail market
a
a
a

*Figure 2*

- when imputing to a parent company the actions of a subsidiary company;[7] and
- when asserting jurisdiction over a parent company based outside the EC by proceeding against a subsidiary established in the EC.[8]

The identification of the relevant economic entity in connection with the analysis of market power as well as the effect of restrictive practices or agreements is, however, the main focus of this article. We address this issue from both a legal and economic perspective. In particular, we wish to explore how the economic analysis of the nature of the firm and the development of the property rights approach to its identification affects our understanding of competition law. Does it matter for the application of merger policy whether we analyse the main subjects of a merger in terms of "a nexus of contracts" or "a collection of assets"? More generally, how is the analysis of market power affected by the way in which we view the firm and define its boundaries?

In the remainder of this article we evaluate the legal and economic criteria for deciding the degree of vertical or horizontal integration of companies and thus their categorisation as an economic entity. We review the rationale for looking at the ownership of assets, ownership of shares, other factors such as employment contracts or trading links, and draw conclusions on the compatibility of the case law of the European Commission and the European Courts with the economic approach to the identification of the firm.

## 2. The definition of the relevant economic entity under EC law

### Undertakings for the purpose of Articles 85 and 86

The firm or relevant commercial entity for the purposes of EC competition law is an "undertaking". This term, which has not been defined in the Treaty, has been interpreted broadly to include any entity carrying on activities of an economic nature, or any collection of

---

7 See *e.g.* Commission Dec 80/1283/EC, *Johnson and Johnson*, OJ 1980 L377/16, in which the Commission imposed fines on Johnson and Johnson for the actions of its subsidiaries where such actions where taken in the common interest of the group, under the control and with the knowledge of the parent company.

8 Case 48/69 *ICI Ltd* v *Commission*, "Dyestuffs" [1972] ECR 619.

resources for economic activities, whether or not for profit.[9] The concept of undertaking is therefore not identical with legal personality for the purpose of company or fiscal law.

In some situations, two or more companies or fiscal entities may be treated as a single undertaking for the purposes of EC competition law. The Court of Justice has held that:

> "in competition law, the term 'undertaking' must be understood as designating an economic unit ... even if in law that economic unit consists of several persons, natural or legal." [10]

The most obvious example of two legally distinct companies which may be equivalent to a single economic unit is a parent and its subsidiary. However, links which are weaker than ownership, such as an agency or sub-contractor relationship, may also give rise to the issue of potential unity.

## Article 85

The concept of an undertaking has, on the whole, been consistently interpreted in the application of Article 85. From the decisions of the Commission and the case law of the European Courts relating to this Article, it can be deduced that the criteria for establishing economic unity and, therefore, the exact boundaries of the undertaking is control, either legal or *de facto*. The Commission and the European Courts take account of any shareholding of one entity in the other, asset ownership links, the composition of management boards and the extent to which one entity influences the commercial actions of the other.

The primary indicator of control and unity is a shareholding of over 50%. Such a shareholding justifies a presumption of control. However, whether this presumption can be retained will depend on the facts and the degree of influence of the parent company over its subsidiary. In *Centrafarm* v *Sterling*[11] the Court held that the allocation of tasks by a parent company between its subsidiaries that were dependent on it and had *no real freedom to determine their course of action* could not infringe Article 85(1) as it did not involve two companies. Similarly in *Viho Europe BV* v *Commission*[12] the Court of First Instance held:

---

9   Case 41/83 *Italy* v *Commission* [1985] ECR 873.
10 Judgment in Case 170/83 *Hydrotherm Geratebau* v *Compact* [1984] ECR 2999 at 3016.
11 [1974] ECR 1147.
12 T-102/92 at para 51.

> "Where the subsidiary, although having a separate legal personality, does not freely determine its conduct on the market but carries out the instructions given to it directly or indirectly by the parent company by which it is wholly controlled, Article 85(1) does not apply to the relationship between the subsidiary and the parent company with which it forms an economic unit."

By contrast, in *Bodson v Pompes Funèbres*[13], the Court of Justice held that the mere fact that an undertaking belonged to a group was not decisive and that regard had to be given to whether the undertakings pursue the same market strategy as the parent. Unified conduct was held to be an important element in evidencing control.

A shareholding of 50% or less is more problematic than a larger shareholding as there are no grounds for a presumption of control. In such cases control may be established on the facts and evidence, including evidence of unified conduct. In *Gosme/Martell-DMP*[14], the Commission established the independence of DMP, a 50/50 subsidiary of Gosme and Martell, based on the independent actions of DMP which:

(1) distributed brands other than those of its parent companies;

(2) relied on its own sales force; and

(3) independently concluded contracts with buying syndicates in France.

In *IJsselcentrale*[15], SEP, a joint venture between four Dutch electricity companies, argued that it, and the four parent companies constituted a single economic entity because they were components in "one indivisible public electricity supply company". The Commission, however, held that the generators were not part of one legal group and there was no unified conduct between them. On this basis it held that the parents were not an economic unit. SEP was also not a unit with any of the parents as control of SEP was shared between all of them.

In *Shell v Commission*[16], the Court of First Instance defined an economic unit as:

> "a unitary organisation of personal, tangible and intangible elements which pursues a specific economic aim on a long-term basis and can contribute to the commission of an infringement of the kind referred to in that provision."

---

13 Case 30/87 *Bodson v Pompes Funèbres* [1988] ECR 2479 at 2513.
14 OJ 1991 L185/23.
15 Commission Dec (91/50/EEC) OJ 1991 L28/32.
16 [1992] ECR II-757 at para 311.

Although this definition makes no direct reference to control, the requirement of a *unitary organisation of personal, tangible and intangible elements* is similar to asset and possibly management links that result in control. This definition also focuses on the joint pursuance of a specific economic aim that is likely to lead to unified conduct.

Although unified conduct may be evidence of control and therefore of unity, it may also be evidence of an agreement to follow the same commercial policy rather than compete. It is, therefore, difficult to distinguish between a cartel and an economic entity if the relevant test is merely unified conduct.[17] The validity of this element alone as the determining factor without control is, therefore, doubtful in the application of Article 85.

Contractual control may be sufficient to establish unity, without the need for ownership links. An agent may be treated as a unit with its principal. This will depend on the function of the agent. It will usually be the case where the agent is integrated into the principal's undertaking, acting as an auxiliary of its principal in the negotiation of business deals. This may be evidenced by the degree of risk assumption.[18] However, if the agent acts on a non-exclusive basis[19] or bears part of the financial risk[20], it may be considered to act as an independent trader. Different aspects of a commercial relationship may be assessed according to different principles. In *ARG/Unipart*[21], the agreement was held to fall outside Article 85(1) insofar as Unipart agreed to promote ARG branded spare parts for a commission but with no assumption of commercial risk. In this respect, Unipart was held to be acting as the agent of ARG. However, Article 85(1) could apply to the rest of the agreement. Unity can therefore be limited to specific commercial policies or activities controlled by the principal.

---

17 It would also be difficult to distinguish between joint and single dominance as discussed further below. This could be problematic in that in the former case it might be possible to establish a breach of Article 85 resulting from the concerted practices of the undertakings with the duopolistic or oligopolistic position. In the latter case Article 85 would not apply. Any challenge of the actions of the economic unit concerned would have to be on the basis of Article 86.

18 The Commission's Notice on Commercial Agency of 1962 implied that the assumption of risk was the decisive factor. However, case law of the European Court of Justice suggests that the auxiliary nature of the agent's function is more important.

19 Case 311/85 *VZW Vereniging van Vlaamse Reisbureaus v VZW Sociale Dienst van Plaatselijke en Gewest Overheidsdienten* [1987] ECR 3801.

20 Case C-266/93 *Volkswagen AG/VAT.*

21 Commission Dec 88/84/EEC, OJ 1988 L45/34.

## Article 86

An assessment under Article 86 involves:

(1) the identification of the company to which the decision should be addressed; and

(2) the determination of the boundaries of the entity whose market power should be assessed, that is to say whether the market strength of related or commercially linked companies should be relevant to the assessment of the strength of the company carrying out the activities in question.

In determining the addressee of its decision, the Commission's practice has not always been consistent. In cases where a subsidiary has abused its dominant position, the Commission has, on occasions, issued the relevant decision against the parent, attributing the policies to the parent.[22] The issue considered is not always overall control over business strategy (although this was the test in *Metro*[23]) but responsibility for individual actions. Whether the abuse should be attributed to the parent is a question of fact in each case. However, the Commission has not always taken action against the parent even when the parent's involvement has been supported by evidence.[24]

Where the Commission takes a narrow view of the addressee of the decision (a subsidiary rather than the parent), it has to consider whether to take account of the activities of related undertakings. This will depend on whether the structural links will, on the facts, have a material influence on a company's position in the relevant market. In *Michelin*, the Court of Justice accepted that the advantages which Michelin NV derived from belonging to a group of undertakings operating throughout the world did have an influence on market power within the Netherlands. However, it rejected the Commission's reliance on the world-wide position of *Hoffman-La Roche* in pharmaceuticals and vitamins in support of a finding of dominance in various specific markets for vitamins.[25]

The application of Article 86 to situations of joint dominance does not focus on the establishment of a single economic entity but on the establishment of minimum ties between the undertakings concerned

---

22 *General Motors* [1975] ECR 1367.
23 Case 75/84 *Metro-SB-Grossmärkte GmbH* v *Commission* [1986] ECR 3021.
24 *BMW Belgium*, OJ 1978 246/33.
25 Case 85/76 *Hoffman-La Roche* v *Commission* [1979] ECR 461.

which lead to unity of action. The question then arises whether such situation is best dealt with under Article 85 as a concerted practice between independent economic entities or a joint dominant position which may be abused by the undertakings concerned. In practice, both Treaty Articles are often relied upon simultaneously by the Commission to terminate competition distortions that may result from such a situation.

## Undertakings in merger analysis

Under the Merger Regulation there are two steps in the assessment of a concentration (mirroring the two steps in Article 86 cases outlined above):

(1) The determination of the existence of a concentration between two or more undertakings on the basis of Article 3. According to Article 3, the concentration will include those companies which have merged or the undertaking which acquires control over another and that other undertaking. This Article helps to decide the relevant jurisdiction and leads on to (2).

(2) The competitive assessment of the concentration (identified in accordance with Article 3) under Article 2. Article 2(1) further specifies that the appraisal of the concentration should take account of, among other matters, the structure of the markets and the market position of the undertakings concerned.

Article 3 of the Merger Regulation states clearly that a concentration consists of the combination of the activities of previously independent undertakings resulting in the creation of a common economic unit. In its Notice on the Notion of a Concentration[26], the Commission states that:

> "a prerequisite for the determination of a common economic unit is the existence of a permanent, single economic management."[27]

As in the application of Article 85, control plays an essential role. Control is defined in Article 3(3) of the Merger Regulation:

---

26 OJ 1994 C385/5.
27 Para 7.

"control shall be constituted by rights, contracts or any other means which either separately or in combination and having regard to the considerations of fact or law involved confer the possibility of exercising decisive influence on an undertaking, in particular by:

(a) ownership or the right to use all or part of the assets of an undertaking;

(b) rights or contracts which confer decisive influence on the composition, voting or decisions of the organs of an undertaking."

The tests for the determination of the undertakings forming part of the concentration are therefore similar to the tests applied in the definition of the relevant undertaking for the purposes of Article 85: control resulting from ownership or the ability to influence the commercial behaviour of the other.

Under the Merger Regulation the Commission must then, under Article 2(1), consider the structure of the markets and determine the market position of the undertakings concerned. This usually entails assessing the extent of the activities of each entity. It allows the calculation of market shares that are an important indicator of market power. The aggregation of activities should logically take account of the "control" test established by Article 3 of the Merger Regulation and the case law relating to Articles 85 and (somewhat less consistently) 86.

Past practice of the Commission in merger control cases supports this view. For example, in merger decisions, the Commission has almost always considered control (*i.e.* the possibility of exercising decisive influence) as the relevant test for the aggregation of market shares. In *Fortis/CGER*[28], the Commission stated clearly that, in the absence of the ability to exercise a decisive influence (which, it held, could take the form of joint control), market shares should not be aggregated for the purpose of the competitive assessment.[29]

In *Kvaerner/Trafalgar*[30], the Commission decided not to aggregate the market shares of Kvaerner and its competitor AMEC. This was so because the Commission found that Kvaerner did not exercise control over AMEC.[31]

In another, more recent and more controversial case, *Kesko/Tuko*[32], the Commission assessed the concentration between two companies

---

28 Case No IV/M342.
29 Paras 27 and 31.
30 Case No IV/M731.
31 Para 6.
32 Case No IV/M784. This case is currently the subject of an annulment application before the Court of First Instance ( Case T– 22/97).

primarily active in the procurement of goods for sale to independent retailers. It aggregated the market shares of the retailer customers and attributed them to the upstream wholesale entities, arguing that:

> "In view of the above elements, i.e. agreements within the K group [between Kesko and its retailer customers], the organisational characteristics, ownership of business premises and financial commitment, it is appropriate to consider Kesko, including the K retailers, as a centrally planned, structural feature of the Finnish retail market."[33]

The Commission rejected the arguments that the various explicit and implicit ties between the wholesale company, Kesko, and the retailers who originally established Kesko varied for each individual retailer and did not amount to control evidencing a single economic unit. It also rejected evidence of lack of uniform conduct. It held that the amount of purchases of K retailers from Kesko and (minority) shareholding links between the K retailers and Kesko justified treatment as a single entity and market share aggregation.

The above case contrasts with *SPAR/Dansk Supermarked*.[34] In that case, an integrated wholesaler/retailer – the Spar group – proposed to set up a retail joint venture with another retailer – the Dansk Supermarked group. The Dansk Supermarked group would transfer to the joint venture its discount retail stores in Germany and would withdraw from this geographic market. The Spar group would continue its activities in Germany. Although the Spar group would hold 50% of the shares of the joint venture and the joint venture would have the option to purchase from the Spar group, the Commission did not consider that it was appropriate to treat the joint venture and the Spar group as a single unit. It held that the purchase by the joint venture of goods from its parent was a co-operative element of the transaction. It considered that it was not even necessary to examine the extent to which the joint venture would participate in the co-operative purchasing system of the Spar group. It held that:

> "Within the framework of the Merger Control Regulation, this cooperative purchasing is an element that must be distinguished from the structural change brought about by the establishment of the joint undertaking."

---

33 Para 66.
34 Case No IV/M179.

Just as agreements between separate companies which are part of the same economic unit do not fall within Article 85(1), further integration between parts of an economic unit does not constitute a merger. This was the case in *Coca-Cola Enterprises/Coca-Cola & Schweppes Beverages Ltd*[35] where the Commission declined to assess the competition implications of the purchase of 49/51% by CCE of the shares in its UK bottling and distribution organisation because it considered that this transaction did not affect the control that CCE already had over CCSB. Without a change in control, the Merger Regulation did not apply. Nevertheless, the Commission looked at the issue of dominance in the relevant market for colas and suggested that there were competition issues under Articles 85 and 86 rather than the Merger Regulation.

Unity in merger analysis, as in analysis under Article 85, is not conditional upon share ownership but does require control. Such control could result from a franchise agreement where the franchisor determines the commercial policy of the franchisees, as was the case in *Promodes/BRMC*.[36] Arguably in such a case it would therefore not be appropriate to assess the agreements between the franchisor and franchisee in the light of Article 85 as there is unity. However, the existence of a block exemption Regulation providing franchises with automatic exemption from the prohibition of Article 85(1) if they meet the conditions of the regulation implies that *prima facie* such agreements fall within this Article.

## Conclusions on legal criteria

The analysis of a given set of arrangements between companies may be considered either under Article 85 or Article 86 (or potentially both) depending on whether the activities are considered part of a single economic entity. The application of the Merger Regulation is similarly affected by this crucial distinction.

The legal criteria for assessing whether or not a system of contractual and ownership relations between two legal entities amounts to that of a single economic entity for the purpose of competition law vary depending on the instrument of EU competition law being employed.

---

35 Case No IV/M794, OJ 1997 L218/15.
36 Case No IV/M242

In Article 85 cases unity is clearly based on the notion of control in the form of decisive influence over commercial behaviour and the consequential manifestation of unified conduct in the market.

In Article 86 cases the Community institutions must identify the entity responsible for the behaviour and then assess the strength of the legal entity in question. The Commission sometimes attributes behaviour to the parent and sometimes to the subsidiary without great consistency. The test here appears to be responsibility rather than control. Where the Commission takes a narrow approach to the definition of the relevant entity it will sometimes take account of the strength of group/related companies if it believes this will have a material influence on the position of the legal entity. The case law of Article 86 often avoids the issue of the relevant economic entity by narrowly defining the market. This effectively allows for consideration of a limited scope of activities of the company concerned and avoids the need to determine the separate boundaries of the economic unit in question.

Assessments under Article 86 are complicated by the theory of joint dominance. Under this theory parties are treated as commercially linked by unity of interest leading to unity of action. The question then arises how to distinguish between joint dominance and concerted action.

In merger control the major element for the determination of a concentration is control. This test has also been applied, although not completely consistently, in the attribution of the market shares of one legal entity to another. This is of some considerable importance. If separate legal entities with close contractual ties are considered to be one economic unit, the whole of their activities will be taken into account in the assessment of dominance and the calculation of the market shares of the merging parties. If third companies with which the merging parties have contracts are not part of one economic unit with the merging companies, the activities of these third companies should not be attributed to the merging parties in the assessment of the market position of the undertakings concerned. Rather these links are to be analysed as part of the effect of the concentration on competition. This subtle distinction is crucial as it forces the Commission to deal with the effects on competition rather than relying on the much cruder structural market share test for merger control.

# 3. Economic criteria for establishing the boundaries of the firm

How does economic theory deal with the question of the boundary of the firm? What are the relevant concepts and what are the criteria used to draw the line between inter-firm transactions or relationships and intra-firm activities? In particular, do the economic concepts support the legally relevant criteria of control and uniform conduct?

## The history of the theory of the firm

In his classic paper on the nature of the firm, Coase (1937) asked two questions:

(1) Why do firms exist?

(2) What determines their size and the scope of their activities?

He took as given that firms exist and that they could be easily identified. He did not therefore ask the question how to decide when a particular organisational structure or set of arrangements between economic agents constitutes a firm and when a set of arrangements between economic agents represented a market transaction. For him this was obvious. A market transaction used the price mechanism and a firm-internal allocation of resources did not. Correspondingly, the main justification for the existence of firms had to be found in the cost of using the market relative to the cost of allocating resources through managerial authority. Coase's seminal contribution of introducing transaction costs into economics was widely acknowledged and yielded him the Nobel Prize. He is credited for having dared to ask a much neglected question about a key actor in the modern economy.

The subsequent literature on the theory of the firm developed only slowly but essentially followed Coase in deepening our understanding of the reasons for organising activities within a firm rather than through the market.[37] Yet his approach was also found to be deficient. For one thing, firms do not exclusively rely on managerial decision-making but make extensive use of internal markets and transfer prices.

---

37 See Alchian/Demsetz (1972) who identified more efficient monitoring within a system of team production, whereas Klein/Crawford/Alchian (1978) and Williamson (1975, 1985) focused on hold-up problems in market transactions which act as an *ex-ante* disincentive for investment into complimentary assets

Firm-internal contracts between parts of a firm are also often formulated in a similar way to those employed in market transactions. Most importantly, however, Coase did not manage to explain how managerial decision-making power is truly distinctive from the competitive forces of a market transaction. Parties to a contractual exchange can use the courts and enforce mutual obligations, but the same is true of employees who are in dispute with their employer. As a result of such criticisms, Jensen/Meckling (1976) even declared the question of the economic justification of a firm practically meaningless because firms were merely a legal fiction and needed to be understood simply as a nexus of contracts. This definition of the nature of the firm as a collection of contracts with a standard form and a legal identity became widely accepted. It did not matter whether an organisation was called a firm or not; the economic substance of the set of contracts mattered, not the organisational form in which they were arranged.

This popular view of the firm did not go unchallenged. Modern industrial organisation theory, chiefly through the contributions of Grossman and Hart (1986) and Hart and Moore (1988, 1990), has provided a more fundamental justification of the firm which is based on property rights and incomplete contract theory.[38] Compared to the earlier theories of the firm, the new property rights based approach defines the firm as a collection of assets rather than contracts. Firms have an explicit role. Their form – the collection of assets in a single organisation – matters, as well as their substance. Firms are no longer a "legal fiction" but important instruments for achieving economic efficiency. In particular, asset ownership provides important residual control rights.

## Control rights

The ability of firms to maintain residual control rights through the ownership of its assets emerges as the main characteristic of firms that distinguish it from other forms of co–ordination of economic activities. Every form of organisation of economic activities, which seeks to exploit specialisation through the division of labour, requires a co–ordinating mechanism. Co–ordination is always necessary, whether in a system of market exchange between consumers and suppliers or

---

38 See Hart (1995) for a fuller treatment of the recent theory and a discussion of established theories.

within a firm where managers are responsible for organising the allocation of resources.

Inevitably, there are disputes and these require resolution. Disputes, which arise in economic relationships, can easily be resolved if the dissatisfied customer can turn to an alternative supplier and go and shop elsewhere. But not every business relationship is as simple as that between the grocer and his customers. Employment relationships are generally more complicated and walking away is not always as easy, as alternative employment may not be as easy to come by. Similarly, suppliers of specialised equipment to a manufacturer would not wish to lose their customers over a single dispute and, by the same token, the manufacturer may rely on his supplier for essential components and would not be able to find an alternative supplier at the drop of a hat. Such a relationship therefore needs to be governed by a system of agreements (informal or formal) that provides the right incentives for both parties to continue a fruitful relationship which benefits them both.

In many millions of market transactions these formal or informal agreements are sufficient to organise the production or exchange of goods and services. Not all relationships can, however, be efficiently regulated by prior agreement. There are always problems that cannot be foreseen and which require an ex post resolution. There are also agreements which cannot be enforced because it cannot be safely established whether a party did or did not meet its obligations under the agreement. In a world of such incompleteness of contracts, alternative mechanisms to control an economic activity are required. Firms that rely on managerial discretion (fiat) can offer a more effective co-ordination mechanism. Management hierarchies within a firm provide a means of resolving the problem of co-ordination of many relationships. The firm provides management with essential control rights to facilitate the allocation of resources and exchange of intermediate goods and services. This does not mean that managerial control is perfect or without costs. It merely says that in some situations a firm-internal organisation of production and exchange may be more efficient. These efficiencies are achieved through a set of control rights.

There is one case study from the economic literature of the theory of the firm that illustrates this point well: General Motors and Fisher Body.[39] This case dates back to the 1920s when Fisher Body supplied car bodies to GM. In 1926 GM decided to buy Fisher Body. The

---

39 See Klein/Crawford/and Alchian (1978) for a full discussion; Hart (1989) for a more recent review of the debate.

reasons behind GM's actions and their consequences for the productivity and investment incentives of the respective managers and workers became the subject of debate. Klein *et al* (1978) argued that it was the organisational capital that GM wanted to acquire. It was seen to be important for GM to resolve the problem of dealing with unforeseen contingencies, such as unexpected demand surges that would have given Fisher Body's management the opportunity to negotiate better prices, with GM unable to say no. In effect, lack of ownership and control over the equipment and machinery of Fisher Body, combined with the impossibility of contractually agreeing every contingency in advance, left GM in an exposed position. Control rested with the owners of Fisher Body and its managers. By buying Fisher Body GM became the owner of its physical assets and other intangible assets that are inextricably tied up with the making of car bodies. The acquisition of assets and their associated control rights helped GM to get around the hold-up problems of the previous market-based contractual relationship with one of its main suppliers.

## Asset ownership

The GM/Fisher Body case study suggests the source of managerial decision-making power and how firms can create control rights. It is the ownership of physical assets that provides the missing link to explain the superior form of control within a firm. Managerial authority stems from the ability to withdraw a physical asset or reallocate it to an alternative activity. If the manager could not do that then his power and control over a productive activity would be much less significant. Hart (1995) considers this issue:

> "Why does ownership of physical or non-human assets matter? The answer is that ownership is a source of power when contracts are incomplete? Given that a contract will not specify all aspects of usage in every contingency, who has the right to decide about missing usages? According to the property rights approach, it is the owner of the asset in question who has this right. That is, the owner of an asset has residual control rights over that asset: the right to decide all usages of the asset in any way not inconsistent with a prior contract, custom, or law."

What kind of assets are relevant for providing these essential control rights? Hart (1989: 1766) lists the types of assets that in his view would help to identify a firm:

- machines; buildings or locations;
- cash; inventories;
- client lists; patents; copyrights.
- other rights and obligations embodied in outstanding contracts.

Not all these assets necessarily provide significant residual control rights to their owners. When determining the value of integration of up and downstream activities such as those of a car supplier and a car manufacturer, it is the machines plus patents that are the most important assets allowing the integrated process to be controlled. In the film industry, control was associated with the "studio" that owned stars, scripts and production facilities. Today, the production of a major budget film is a unique undertaking which relies on the value of the creative stars who are the main assets in film–making. But, as they are human assets and not physical assets, it is impossible for a "studio" to own them and control the production of the film. Rather it is the other way around. The stars own the films and then employ production facilities and distributors to produce and market them.

Another situation can be found in retailing. Historically, retailers were independent entrepreneurs who owned their shops, including the inventories and sometimes the premises they worked and lived in. Retailers were supplied by independent wholesalers. This world of independent firms who transact with each other over the market has changed radically. Today, retailing is increasingly dominated by large multiple retailers who own chains of retail outlets and are integrated upstream into wholesaling. The retail chains are uniformly branded and operated by employees rather than independent entrepreneurs. The logistics and inventories are centrally managed. In other words, the boundaries of the retailing modern firm are generally drawn rather wide.

## Conclusions on economic criteria

The modern economic theory of the firm considers firms as a collection of assets which provide control rights to their owners in a world of incomplete contracts. Essentially, the theory focuses on two key elements:

- control rights (in particular residual control rights); and
- asset ownership (particularly ownership of complimentary physical assets).

These two criteria help to distinguish the firm from other forms of resource allocation, namely those based on market transactions whose control mechanisms are inferior even though their incentive structures may sometime be superior.

## 4. The compatibility of the legal and economic approaches to the firm

The boundary of the firm is a matter of business strategy as well as commercial law. The firm-internal organisation of economic activities may bring benefits over and above those achievable if the same activities were organised between independent agents through contracts or other less formal market arrangements. EC competition law recognises the distinction between firm-internal resource allocation and resource allocation over the market. In particular, the case law of Article 85(1) reviewed in this article demonstrates an awareness of the need to distinguish between firm-internal and external relationships. Similarly, Article 3 of the Merger Regulation provides a clear definition of the undertakings relevant for the assessment of competitive effects of a concentration. The exception is the case law on Article 86 where the definition of the relevant economic entity has not been addressed in any great detail or with a large degree of consistency.

What can we say about the comparison of the relevant criteria used in economics and in law to determine the boundary of the firm? Are these criteria similar and, more importantly, are they compatible? Does economic theory support the criteria used in EU competition law?

### Control rights

At first sight it appears that there is a large degree of commonality between the two sets of criteria. The notion of control is important for both the legal and economic approaches. The notion of control in the law is equated with the exercise of decisive influence over the behaviour of another company or part of a business (whether legally independent or not). The ownership of assets or the rights to use the assets is one of the elements conferring control, as stated in Article 3(3) of the Merger Regulation. This coincides with the notion of control rights in the modern theory of the firm.

However, the economic notion of ownership of complementary assets which give rise to residual control rights is more precise than the test applied in EC competition law. The notion of decisive influence becomes clearer if the Commission must positively ascertain whether the economic entities under investigation are subject to the same source of residual control rights backed by asset ownership.

The economic approach narrows down the types of asset that are important in creating effective control. It is not sufficient merely to own assets that can easily be bought on the open market and installed without much effort. This type of asset does not provide much in terms of control rights. Major complimentary assets include dedicated equipment, factories and brands. Against this precise notion of the source of control rights, EC case law qualifies the value of the primary indicator – a controlling shareholding of at least 50% – and introduces the notion of unified conduct.

## Unified conduct

In Article 85 and merger control case law, unified conduct constitutes evidence of control. In Article 86 cases, unified conduct is considered in the allocation between parent companies and undertakings of responsibility for actions. It is not used for establishing unity but responsibility.

The use of unified conduct as a criterion for unity is problematical in that it fails to distinguish between the unified conduct of members of a cartel and the unified conduct of entities under the control of another entity. Similarly, vertical restrictions between manufacturers and distributors or distributors and retailers may be designed to lead to, unified conduct on the market place. Distributors or retailers may be expected to follow a common format when displaying their goods for promotion. They are also often expected to invest in marketing and promotion activities along with other distributors or retailers. This is in the interests of both parties (and usually in the interests of consumers) but we would not usually call this unified behaviour that of a single economic entity. It merely shows a high degree of co–ordination between independent firms which operate at different levels of the market but share a common interest in promoting a product. Unified conduct is not, therefore, a sufficiently distinctive criterion for determining the boundaries of a firm.

This point can be further illustrated when considering the relationship between central management and franchisees. A franchised retailer network has many of the properties of a single firm, such as uniform branding for the outlet (and its products) and centralised logistics. Yet the manager of the individual outlet operates the shop independently on his or her own account. The franchisee is not, however, completely independent and cannot act with complete autonomy. Usually, there is a long complex franchise contract that ties the retailer to the franchiser in many ways. The franchise agreement sets down much of what an independent retailer would determine himself: selection of goods, presentation of product, appearance and fit-out of the shop, etc.

What, then, is the relevant economic boundary of the franchise network? If we take the list of assets quoted above and try to allocate them to the franchisee and franchiser respectively, we will probably find that they fall equally between the two. The franchiser holds all the trade marks in the brand and the own brand goods that are sold, often exclusively. The franchisee will usually own the cash book and employ staff. Then there are assets such as the shop lease, the fixtures and fittings, which could be owned by either. The more assets that are owned by the franchiser, the more control rests with the franchiser and less with the outlet manager, the franchisee. But the situation is far from clear cut and the best we can do is to evaluate the situation on a case-by-case basis.

## Assessment of market structure and competition

If we accept the overriding criterion for determining the boundaries of the firm to be the scope and reach of residual control rights, secured by ownership of key assets, then this has significant implications for the assessment of market structure. The application of European competition law in the areas of mergers is well known to be heavily dependent on the use of market shares as indicators of market structure and dominance.[40] Merger Regulation case law discussed above shows that market shares of legally independent firms should only be aggregated if the firms are considered as an economic unit. There are, however, some cases where this rule has not been observed. Such cases convolute two important separate steps of the assessment of

---

40 See Neven, Nuttall and Seabright (1993).

competition under the Merger Regulation: the assessment of market structure; and the assessment of effects of the concentration on competition. These two steps are conceptually different.

As a result of the slightly different tests applied in different circumstances there appear to be inconsistencies in the Commission's practice. Under merger control, a franchise may be treated as an integrated entity. However, the very existence of a block exemption granting exemption to certain franchise agreements under Article 85(3) implies that, *prima facie*, franchises are treated as agreements between non-integrated entities falling within Article 85(1). Maybe these apparent inconsistencies are the result of different factual circumstances. However, it is not always clear from the Commission's decisions what these differences could be.

## 5. Conclusion

This article has explored the economic rationale behind the identification of the relevant economic entity in EC competition law. Of particular interest is the assessment of vertical relationships between legally independent entities that, nevertheless, work in close collaboration with each other. This collaboration takes place through implicit or explicit agreements. The question is whether such agreements should be considered as firm-internal and, therefore, non-restrictive of competition. The comparison of the legal and economic criteria shows a mixed picture. The central legal criteria of control and decisive influence are consistent with the economic criterion of residual control rights. The property rights approach emphasises residual control rights that are provided by asset ownership and this supports the legal notion of control. In fact, the economic rationale helps to clarify the legal criterion. The ownership of physical assets rather than contractual agreements or other rights becomes the key indicator of control rights.

The review of case law has, however, also thrown up a second legal criterion which finds less support in economic theory: unified conduct. Particularly as concerns vertical relationships between suppliers and distributors/retailers this is not a clear and unambiguous indicator of firm-internal control. Uniform conduct or common objective are the rationale for many vertical agreements between independent firms and cannot readily be assumed to be the exclusive characteristic of firms. Furthermore, lack of uniform conduct is not conclusive of independence.

Finally, the aggregation by the Commission of market shares for the assessment of actual or potential market power has been shown to be inconsistent with the concept of the boundary of the firm. Only if the relevant economic entity has been clearly identified is it justifiable to include in the market share indicator all activities associated with the firm. If the boundaries are drawn more tightly and relationships between manufacturers and distributors are considered arms length and contractual, then the allocation of the distributors' market shares to the manufacturer would be misleading. The existence of contractual or informal links between firms may give rise to significant effects on competition. But these effects should be analysed separately from the structural analysis of the markets affected. Contractual relationships are not of the same nature and strength as those that are based on ownership. To ignore these real differences in commercial life would be to take the law beyond the justification of economics.

Sarah Beeston
Tom Hoehn

## Bibliography

Alchian, A, and Demsetz, H, "Production, information costs and economic organization" (1972) *American Economic Review* 62(5), 777-795.

Bellamy & Child, *Common Market Law of Competition*, 4th ed and 1st Supp to 4th ed.

Butterworths, *Competition Law*, last updated 1997.

Coase, R H, "The nature of the firm" (1937) *Economica*, 4 pp 386-405.

Grossman, S and Hart, O, "The costs and benefits of ownership: a theory of vertical and lateral integration" (1986) *Journal of Political Economy*, 94, pp 691-719.

Hart, O, *Firms, Contracts and Financial Structure* Oxford, Clarendon Press (1995).

Hart, O, "An economist's perspective on the theory of the firm" (1989) *Columbia Law Review*, 89, pp 1757-1774.

Hart, O and Moore, J, "Property rights and the nature of the firm" (1990) *Journal of Political Economy*, 98, pp 1119-1158.

Jensen, M and Meckling, W, "Theory of the firm: managerial behaviour, agency costs and ownership structure" (1976) *Journal of Financial Economics*, Vol 3, pp 305-360.

Klein, B, Crawford, R and Alchian, A, "Vertical integration, appropriable rents and the competitive contracting process" (1978) *Journal of Law and Economics*, 21(2), pp 297-326.

Neven D, Nuttall S and Seabright P, *Merger in Daylight – the Economics and Politics of European Merger Control* (1993) CEPR, London.

Williamson, O, *The Economic Institutions of Capitalism* (1985) New York, Free Press.

Williamson, O, *Markets and Hierarchies: Analysis and Antitrust Implications* (1975) New York, Free Press.

# Competitive Regulation of Digital Pay TV

## Dr Cento Veljanovski

The author is Managing Partner of Case Associates, the economics and management consulting practice providing advisory, strategic, economic and regulatory services; No 1 Northumberland Avenue, Trafalgar Square, London WC2N 5BW. Telephone (44-171) 376 4418; cento@globalnet.co.uk

*European Economics & Law*

Palladian Law Publishing Ltd

# Competitive Regulation of Digital Pay TV

Pay TV is attracting increasing attention from competition authorities and regulators. In the past the expansion of television channels was limited by spectrum shortages, mostly due to government intervention, which created monopoly positions. Digital television removes this "bottleneck", and provides the basis for the convergence of previously distinct industries and products. Yet while the merging of telecommunications, media and computing into new products and services has not created one giant communications marketplace, it has led to new concerns requiring detailed regulation, or so it is claimed. One central concern is that a small number of media and telecommunications companies are gaining dominant positions in delivery, key programme rights (movies, sport), and "gateways" for digital pay TV. These concerns are heightened by the belief that the formative stages of digital television will influence its development and eventual market structure (sometimes called "path dependence"). In this article regulatory activity in three areas – digital pay TV alliances, delivery platforms, and conditional access – are examined.

## 1. Digital evolution

### Compression and convergence

In most European countries television is transmitted in analogue form and received on PAL television sets. Analogue transmission is based on waves and consumes considerable spectrum bandwidth. This has meant that with the expansion in channels and services, capacity limits have been reached on many delivery platforms. In the United Kingdom broadband cable networks, which have capacity for up to 50 analogue video channels, have reached their limits with the increasing number of new pay TV channels unable to gain carriage. A similar situation exists in Germany, the Netherlands and other countries. The introduction of digital transmission will remove this bottleneck, greatly increasing the carriage capacity of all delivery systems.

Digital transmission takes the form of a bitstream of 1s and 0s. All content is converted into a common binary language and transmitted over different delivery systems. All computers and CD players are digital, as are an increasing number of telephone and mobile systems. In Europe television is moving to digital transmission including many of the established terrestrial channels (Table 1).

| Country | DTT (launch date) | Satellite DTH (satellite) | Cable (Major operators) |
|---|---|---|---|
| UK | Ondigital BBC, ITV, C4 (1998) | Sky Digital (1998) *(Astra IE)* | Cable & Wireless (1999) NTL (1999) Telewest (1999) |
| Germany | (2001/02) | DFI (1996) *(Astra IE)* Premiere (1997) *(Astra IE)* | DT |
| Spain | (1999) | Canal Satelite Digital (1996) *(Astra IE)* Via Digital Spain (1997) *(Hispasat)* | Cable Antena (1996) |
| France | (2000) | AB Sat (1996) *(Eutelsat II - Hotbird)* Canal Satellite Numerique (1996) *(Astra IE)* TPS (1996) *(Eutelsat II - Hotbird)* | Campagnie Generale Video- communications (1997), Lyonnaise Cable (1997), France Telecom Cable (1997) |
| Italy | (2002) | D+ (1996) , *(Eutelsat II - Hotbird)* Blue Stream (1998) | Stream (1996) |

*Source: Screen Digest, Oct 1997, Cable & Satellite Yearbook 1997*

*Table 1: Digital pay TV platforms*

Two words are associated with the impending digital revolution – *compression* and *convergence*.

The potential of digitisation has been recognised for some time. It was not used earlier because it consumed a large amount of bandwidth. A standard digital television programme typically requires 15 times the bandwidth of an equivalent analogue transmission. This is no longer the case because of advances in digital compression techniques. For example, satellite systems now have tremendous capacity as a result of digital compression. The present generation of digital satellites are working on compression ratios of 1:4 to 1:10, which means that 4 or 10 video channels respectively can be transmitted on the bandwidth previously used to carry one analogue video channel. Thus, satellites which once offered only 10 channels, hold out the prospect of up to 100 channels.

Digital transmission is leading to a degree of convergence.[1] This is the combining of telecommunications, computing and television sectors to create multimedia platforms. Communications systems, which have traditionally been designed around the carriage of one type of content – voice, music, pictures, or text and data, will soon be able to carry all these. Once digitised, all information is essentially the same; it establishes a common language between communications and computing. Thus, data, video and audio signals combined with computing power can create new services and products. Microsoft's *Encarta* provides a good example – an electronic encyclopaedia in digital format which combines words, sound and pictures on a computer or on-line. It can play passages from operas, or speak to us in foreign languages. Another example of convergence is the Internet. The World Wide Web uses the telephone line to provide all media ranging from text, newspapers, data, computer software, voice telephony, videos and television channels. Using Web browsers these different media can be located, linked and manipulated in the home using the PC keyboard or television keypad.

These technological developments have led to significant supply-side changes. Foremost among these has been the potentional breaking of the delivery bottleneck. Digital transmission significantly increases the capacity available to deliver video and telecommunications via separate networks, or "networks of networks". However, judging by the actions of competition authorities this does not imply that there will be unfettered competition. Developments in telecommunications have seen regulators develop structural market definitions, which assert that other "bottlenecks" and "gateways" are likely to develop.[2] In

---

1 See discussion in "Beyond the telephone, the television and the PC", Oftel, August 1995; "Creating the superhighways of the future: developing broadband communications in the UK", Department of Trade & Industry, Cm 2734, HMSO 1994.
2 C G Veljanovski, "Market definition in telecommunications – the confusing proliferation of competitive standards" (1999) *Computer & Telecommunications Law Review* forthcoming.

*WorldCom/MCI* the EC Commission concluded that the Internet backbone (the large "pipes" carrying Internet traffic) was a "bottleneck" and required the parties to divest MCI's backbone operation.

Secondly, digitalisation has created product innovation. Digital transmission will transform television. It will enable pay per view (ppv) turning the television set into an online video library rather than offering pre-packaged channels at times determined by broadcasting and/or regulators. It offers the possibility of interactive television giving viewers greater choice of how video images are provided, and can be combined with other services such as home shopping, the Internet and so on. The development of these products requires large investments and is surrounded by considerable uncertainty as to whether consumers are prepared to pay for an ever increasing range of products or value television as an active rather than passive medium. Many believe convergence will destroy POT – plain old television. The future, so it is argued, is in multi-media companies combining the production and packaging of content sold in different formats to consumers. In other words, vertically integrated companies providing a one-stop shop packaging of electronic content for separate markets.

## The digital value chain

The digital economy is often represented as a "value chain" of linked activities. The simplest value chain draws a distinction between content and carriage. A more useful one breaks it into five activities – content creation, exploitation of programme rights, programme packaging (channels), delivery, and access/encryption systems. This article ignores content creation, exploitation and packaging, to focus on **delivery** and **payment systems** (conditional access and related activities).

In most countries, pay TV is delivered by analogue satellite, cable and terrestrial wireless networks. In the near future many of these networks

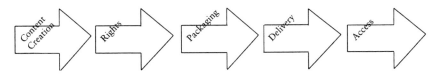

*Table 2: The pay TV chain*

will be in competition with new digital systems using the same means of delivery. Frequently, a channel or video signal uses more than one platform. For example, satellite may be used to network channels across many individual cable systems. In other cases these networks compete head-on for viewers. In the United Kingdom cable, satellite, and digital terrestrial television (DTT) compete directly for viewers. Each has different technical advantages and constraints, and together with the seemingly ceaseless technical advance has led to endless speculation as to which will dominate pay TV. This is discussed in Sections 2 and 3.

Access is an increasing important issue to the pay TV industry (Section 4). Regulators have focused on two main aspects – set-top box and conditional access systems (CAS), and electronic programme guides (EPGs).

CAS lies at the heart of pay TV. In order to receive pay TV an Integrated Receiving Decoder (IRD), often called a decoder or settop box, is needed. The decoder sits on or near the television set and receives the encrypted video channels. This requires a conditional access system (CAS), and a separate billing and subscriber management system (SMS). CAS is a device which operates in much the same way as an *electronic turnstile*, allowing those who have paid to view the pay TV channels, and those who have not to see only a distorted picture. The key that unlocks the decoders currently takes the form of a *smartcard*. Authorised subscribers access programmes through a smartcard which contains algorithms enabling different bundles of programmes to be decoded and viewed, depending on the tiers which the subscriber has purchased. In the future television sets may contain the necessary electronics to remove the need for decoders and smartcards, and will be directly addressable by the pay TV operator.

EPGs are seen by many as critical in a multichannel environment. EPGs are the electronic equivalent of a TV programme guide. They work in the same way as web browsers providing menus and search engines of the programmes, channels and other services. EPGs implement and guide viewers' choice, and hence can be used to influence that choice to the detriment of some channels.

## 2. **Digital alliances**

The Commission has been accused of taking an unduly restrictive view of the competitive process and has blocked several "digital alliances" formed to bear the large costs and risks of creating new digital platforms. The EC Competition Commissioner, Karel van Miert, has denied accusations that he gets out a "bazooka" whenever the words "pay TV alliance" are mentioned. This view in part comes from the statistics. Since the inception of the *Merger Regulation 1989*, the Commission has prohibited 10 concentrations, five in television and of these four concerned pay TV alliances (although three were effectively the same proposal). To this must be added a further prohibition which was avoided when the project was abandoned (Telfonica/Sogecable in Spain), and indirect intervention which forced BSkyB's withdrawal from the winning consortium (DBD in the UK). The Commission argues, in its defence, that this evidence is misleading since over the same period it allowed 20 or so other mergers and joint ventures such as Bertelsmann-CLT (1996), HMG/RTL (1997), BDB (1998), BiB (1998) and TPS (1993).[3]

## EU Merger Decisions

The Commission has blocked several high profile digital alliances in Germany (twice) and the Nordic countries.

In 1994 the EC Merger Taskforce examined the proposed joint venture between Bertelsman, Taurus (owned by the Kirch Gruppe) and Deutsche Telekom (called MSG Media Service Gesellschaft fur Abwicklung von Pay-TV und verbundenen Diensreo) to develop "technical and administrative services" (conditional access, subscriber management, decoder boxes) for a digital pay TV service for Germany. The Commission in *MSG Media Services*[4] concluded that the proposed joint venture would foreclose digital pay TV to competition because it brought together Germany's (then) only pay TV channel (Premiere) owned by Kirch who had a large quantity of pay and other television programme rights, Germany's largest media company Bertelsmann, and the (then) state-owned cable and telephone company Deutsche Telekom. In Germany cable is the main pay TV platform with some 43% of all television households (14 million out of 33 million households) wired to Deutsche Telekom's cable network. As a result, the proposed joint venture involved significant vertical relationships – programming rights,

---

3  J F Pons "The future of broadcasting" paper to Institute of Economic Affairs conference, June 1998. Also P Larouche "EC competition law and the convergence of the telecommunications and broadcasting sectors" (1998) *Telecommunications Policy*, Vol 22, 219-242.
4  Case No IV/M.469.

leasing transponders, conditional access technology, and cable and DTH distribution. The Commission felt that this would have the effect of foreclosing the market to other pay TV operators.

In late 1998, the Commission found itself again investigating a renewed joint venture by the "MSG three", following a period of deep uncertainty in Germany's digital development caused by several abortive alliances (CLT/Kirch, CLT/BSkyB, Kirch/BSkyB), based on incompatible settop boxes, the withdrawal of Bertelsmann, and the poor take-up of Kirch's DF1 digital services. In *Bertelsmann/Kirch/Premiere*[5] and the related *Deutsche Telekom/Betaresearch*[6] mergers, the Commission reaffirmed its earlier position by once again prohibiting the proposed alliance. Today Germany has no pay TV sector to speak of.

In 1995 *Nordic Satellite Distribution (NSD)*[7] the Commission examined a joint venture between two stated-owned PTOs – Norsk Telekom and Tele Danmark – and Kinnevik, a television company which operated the most popular pay TV channel. NSD planned to provide satellite transmission and distribution services via cable networks or direct-to-home (DTH) in the Nordic countries (Sweden, Norway, Denmark and Finland), and develop a common digital encryption system for DTH, SMATV and cable. NSD's objective was to enable each household to use a single settop box irrespective of whether they receive the signal by cable or DTH.

Key:  NT = Norsk Telekom (now Telenor)    TD = Tele Danmark    K = Kinnevik

|  | Norway | Sweden | Finland | Denmark |
|---|---|---|---|---|
| Satellite | NT | NT | NT | NT |
| Transponders | NT | NT/K | NT | NT/K |
| Distribution | NT | K |  | TD |
| Programming | K | K | K | K |

*Table 3: Activities of the parties to NSD joint venture*

The Commission was concerned about the anti-competitive impact of the joint venture in three markets. In the *satellite transponder market* the Commission stated that NSD would acquire a dominant position in

5 Case No. IV/M.993.
6 Case No. IV/M.1027.
7 Case No. IV/M.490.

the market for satellite TV transponder services suitable for Nordic viewers. It stated that through its control over most transponder capacity, links with Kinnevik and links with cable operators, NSD would be able to foreclose other satellite operators from leasing transponders to broadcasters.[8] In the market for *cable delivery* the Commission stated that the creation of NSD would lead to a strengthening of dominant cable positions in Denmark, and would allow NSD to discriminate in favour of its parent companies' cable operations in Sweden and Norway. Finally, the Commission viewed NSD as reducing competition in *satellite DTH distribution* with the result that NSD would be able to foreclose the market through its control of relevant satellite transponder capacity and control over cable. The Commission blocked the merger stating:

> "The operation will have an impact on the affected markets either horizontally or through vertical links created. NSD will after the operation, control an integrated infrastructure for the provision of TV services to the Nordic area as well as the right to transmit some of the most important TV channels in the area".[9]

In effect it narrowed the relevant market because of the vertical links with cable operators:

> "Particularly it should be noted that the positions of the parties in downstream markets (cable networks and distribution) reinforce the dominant position on transponders by deterring potential competitors from broadcasting from other transponders to the Nordic market".[10]

These two decisions show the Commission's reluctance to compromise the prospect of competition, however remote, for the possibility of a rapid launch of new digital pay TV services. This is underpinned by two principal competitive concerns. The first is the view that the relevant market is defined narrowly as pay TV, and perhaps even digital pay TV. Secondly, that alliances which involve vertical links between major owners of programme libraries and delivery systems (satellite and cable), and horizontal links between different delivery systems, foreclosing the sector to others even in countries which have no significant pay TV (discussed in Section 3 in more detail).

---

8   *Ibid*, para 109.
9   *Ibid*, para 71.
10  *Ibid*, para 164.

## Market definition

It is settled that when assessing proposed mergers and joint ventures the Commission is required to define the relevant markets, and to assess the competitive constraints on the merged entity's ability to act independently of its competitors and customers. The EC *Merger Regulation* differs from Article 86 by requiring a forward-looking approach. The difficulty in applying market definition to a product which is not yet available is evident.

In any activity there are different markets – input, retail, wholesale and so on – in which the products and or services regarded as substitutes will differ. Pay TV may compete with free to air (FTA) TV,[11] and other media for some inputs (programming rights) or in the sale of some services (advertising), and in the product market (such as news programmes) but not for others. For each, the range of media regarded as competitive with pay TV will differ.

The EC Commission concluded that pay TV, and even digital pay TV, was a separate product market. In *MSG Media Services* it held that pay and FTA TV did not compete directly, and the premium pay channels (thus excluding subscription services involving the re-transmission of terrestrial and other channels) did not compete with advertiser financed and public television. Two reasons were given – different customers (FTA broadcasters supply advertisers whereas pay TV sells programmes/channels to the viewers) and "conditions of competition" (FTA broadcasters are concerned about audience share and advertising rates whereas pay TV operators cater to the interests of target groups and subscriber prices).

This analysis is hotly contested by many pay TV operators in competition law proceedings. They argue that pay channels compete not only with other pay TV channels but all other television channels, and other forms of video and general entertainment, such as the cinema, and video sales and rentals. Viewers have access to both FTA and pay TV, and allocate their viewing across all channels on the basis of the popularity of programmes at any one time. In order to attract the viewers' attention, the channels will schedule programmes which appeal to viewers and counter-schedule against those channels which threaten their audience shares or profits. The migration of viewers from FTA to pay TV when the latter is introduced together with the attempt

---

11 That is television which is free to the viewer and financially supported by advertising, licence fees and/or general tax revenues.

of FTA broadcasters to block, hamper and constrain pay TV, are frequently cited as evidence that both compete. This *supply response* makes all channels potentially competitive. Thus, *all television* or *all video entertainment*, it is argued, is in the same the relevant market. This is discussed further in a later section.

## Price analysis

This argument simply does not "wash" with competition authorities. The EC Commission, in common with most competition authorities, defines markets in a technical way aimed at assessing the extent to which one form of video entertainment imposes a competitive constraint on another in setting its prices. In EC law this called the "relevant market".

The key to defining the relevant market is the intensity of demand-side substitution between products. The Commission's Relevant Market Notice, like the US Department of Justice/Federal Trade Commission Horizontal Merger Guidelines, makes price competition key to market definition.[12] The Commission believes demand-side substitutability "constitutes the most immediate and effective disciplinary force on the suppliers of a given product, in particular in relation to their pricing decisions". Under the Relevant Market Notice a relevant product market is defined as the range of products, which if under the control of one supplier would enable it to profitably raise price above the prevailing level.[13] The market is defined through an analysis of the smallest group of products which have sufficiently inelastic demand that a hypothetical profit-maximising monopoly supplier of these would be able to impose "a small but significant and nontransitory increase in price". This is alternatively referred to as SSNIP or "hypothetical monopolist" test (although neither of these terms is used in the Notice). A SSNIP is usually taken to be a 5% increase in price, although this

---

12 Notice on the definition of the relevant markets for the purposes of Community competition law 97/C 372/03 (October 1997) and Guidelines on the application of EEC competition rules in the telecommunications sector 91/C 233/02 (September 1991). C G Veljanovski "The economics of the relevant market in EC competition law" (1998) 185 *International Review of Competition Law* 4-10.
13 Ideally market definition should be examined by statistical analysis to find whether the quantity demanded of a product is price elastic in the sense that an increase in price leads to more than a proportionate fall in the quantity demanded thus lowering the supplier's profits. This finding would establish that consumers had choice of substitutable products to which they could turn to defeat any unilateral attempt to increase price.

figure is entirely arbitrary. This would mean that if all pay TV operators (hypothetically) merged they would be able to raise subscription charges above the pre-existing level if pay TV were a self-contained market. If, on the other hand, pay TV was substitutable in the viewer's eyes for FTA channels and other video entertainment, the hypothetical monopolist of pay TV would not be able to raise its price; viewers would simply switch over to the FTA channels!

The difficulty is that this competition law definition of the market remains hypothetical, at least in Europe's formative pay TV markets. Studies of the price sensitivity of pay TV exist in the more mature US market. These are however interesting but of little assistance. They provide estimates of the (absolute) price elasticity of demand for basic cable (defined as the re-transmission of FTA channels) ranging widely from 0.8 to 3.75, *i.e.* anything from no sensitivity to highly elastic demand implying considerable substitution. The upper range of the estimates suggests pay TV competes with other products, although these studies usually do not identify which. It is also the case that premium channels are treated in the United States as part of a wider market competing with video sales and rentals, and to some extent cinema.

The only analysis of pay TV pricing in European regulatory proceedings so far was by the UK Office of Fair Trading (OFT) in its Pay TV Review.[14] The OFT mirrored the EC Commission's finding that pay TV is a separate market, and that premium channels constitute a distinct sub-market. It found that BSkyB had a dominant position in the supply of the key movies and sport premium channels.[15] While the OFT

---

14 The Director General's Review of BSkyB's position in the wholesale pay TV market.

15 Using increasingly narrow "market" definitions BSkyB's share of viewing rises significantly. Its share of total pay TV audience is 50% and it has 70% of DTH subscribers. As one moves to premium channels BSkyB's prominence is more evident rising to nearly 100% of the premium channel markets. The OFT regarded the degree of substitution between pay TV and broadcast TV channels as being insufficient to constrain the wholesale price of BSkyB's premium channels. The OFT concluded that there was evidence that BSkyB was exercising its market power. This relied almost exclusively on a finding that BSkyB was earning excess economic profits consistent with the OFT's observation that there were barriers to entry caused by limited carriage capacity. BSkyB's dominant position was alleged to be due to a number of factors. In particular its first-mover advantages in the premium channel market, its ability to pay more for sports rights, the existence of barriers to entry arising from insufficient analogue transponder capacity, and its control of the conditional access system which gave access to the Astra installed subscriber base all operated to give it market power. The OFT, however, accepted that there was no evidence that BSkyB contrived the SES transponder allocation or that it had denied access to its encryption system. Rather it was asserted that there was a "perception" that BSkyB would make access difficult! However, because of the uncertainty generated by digital television, the OFT offered little apparent remedy other than to negotiate further voluntary undertakings to provide access to its Videocrypt to all on non-discriminatory cost-related published tariff. "BSkyB gives new undertakings to Director General of Fair Trading", OFT News Release No 32/96, 24 July 1996.

examined BSkyB's prices to define the market, its approach was simplistic. Like the Commission in *MSG Media Services*, it looked at whether pay and FTA TV were substitutes by comparing their absolute price differences and the correlation between prices.[16] This clearly was inappropriate since free TV does not have a price, and therefore the conclusion that they were in separate markets is unsurprising. It then suggested that the large increase in subscription charges was supporting evidence that BSkyB had market power. However, to look solely at absolute price increases in a vacuum is unsatisfactory when there have been major quality and quantity improvements over the period in the basic package and in premium channel programming. Prices may diverge or converge because quality alters over time. The OFT's analysis on this point was equivalent to arguing that the price of a bag of oranges can be compared to that of a box of mangoes to come up with a meaningful conclusion about market power. The relevant comparison is to correlate measures of *quality and quantity adjusted prices*.

The OFT expressly rejected the validity on such adjustments which calculate the implicit per channel prices of each package on the grounds that these were sold together. Since the viewer could not buy individual channels the OFT argued that it was invalid to look at implicit per channel prices. However, when this is done a different picture emerges. In the period examined by the OFT, each price rise by BSkyB was accompanied by an increase in the number of channels in its basic tier package (the Multi Channel Package or MCP) and often in premium packages. Over the period 1993-96 the subscription to MCP increased by 71.5% compared to increases of 200.3% for Sky Sports and 50.0% for the Movie channels (Table 4). These increases far exceeded the rate of inflation or the increase in cinema ticket prices. However, for a price increase to indicate market power there must be evidence of a reduction in some (relevant) measure of output. The evidence shows the opposite. Over the period 1993-96 considered by the OFT, the number of channels in the MCP increased from 11 to 30 channels. When the price is adjusted for the number of channels, the implicit price per channel declined by 37.1% compared with the 71.5% increase in basic subscription charges. That is, more choice at a lower per channel price.

---

16 These two types of price analysis are routinely used in practical competition analysis. A wide difference in the price of two products is sometimes taken as indicative that the two products are in different markets since if they were close substitutes the consumer would clearly buy the cheaper one. The positive correlation of prices over time is taken as evidence that the two products are in the same market since they are clearly influenced by the same factors. Both these tests are imperfect but useful parts of an array of tests to provide evidence of substitution.

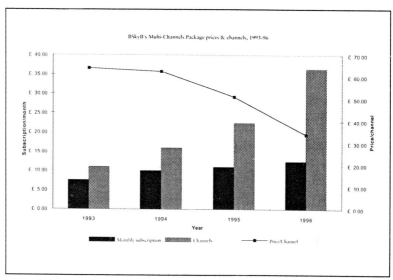

*Table 4*

## Non-price competition

It is axiomatic that in order for digital pay TV to succeed it must show different programming. That is, pay TV and, particular digital television, is a formative or innovative product. A corollary is that the attractiveness and take-up of pay TV will be affected by the nature of the FTA services. If FTA channels provide high quality programming attractive to viewers, then the take-up and pricing of pay TV will, other things being equal, be lower. In more technical parlance, the residual demand curve facing pay TV operators not only alters as a result of the actions of other pay TV operators but FTA television channels. Their actions can reduce or increase demand, and twist the demand curve facing an individual pay operator.

The strength of these supply-side responses depends on commercial and regulatory factors. If FTA channels feel that pay TV operators are making sufficient in-roads into their audiences, which affect advertising revenues, then they will counter-schedule against pay TV. Moreover, both FTA and pay TV compete for high rating material such as sport, and other mass appeal programming. By acquiring such premium programming and scheduling it against, say, a pay sport channel FTA broadcasters can affect not only the price of a sports channel but the pay TV operators total subscriber numbers and penetration rate.

The use of price competition as the sole basis for determining market definition in technologically dynamic industries, such as pay TV, can and has been questioned.[17] A number of grounds have been advanced, which generally reduce to insufficient attention to supply-side substitution possibilities and excessive limited time frames. Some have even suggested that non-price competition should form the basis of any competition law analysis. It is argued that newly introduced products are "experience goods" which must be used in order for consumers to properly evaluate their price-performance characteristics, so that the boundaries of the markets are unknown and certainly fuzzy. As consumers (viewers) are trialling a new product, a price increase of 5% or even 25% may not immediately induce substitution. Thus, a price-based test will result in an excessively narrow market definition, and identification of market power where none genuinely exists.

Professors Jorde and Teece have advocated that the US Merger Guidelines (and by implication the EC approach) be recast in terms of changes in attributes rather than prices:

> "the pertinent question to ask is whether a change in the performance attributes of one commodity would induce substitution to or from another. If the answer is affirmative, then the differentiated products, even if based on alternative technologies, should be included in the relevant product market."[18]

Such a test might ask whether consumers would shift to other products to defeat a 25% lowering of quality in any key performance attribute or whether a new product exhibiting a 25% improvement in a key performance attribute would draw sufficient customers from the old product. If so, the substitute products would be included in the relevant market. Advocates of attribute-based market definition also propose a longer time period within which to evaluate consumer and supplier reaction. Jorde and Teece propose four years compared to the one/two years used by the US Merger Guidelines.

### The evidence

The Commission has observed the importance of supply-side factors. In *MSG Media Services* it agreed that pay TV would find the going

---

17 For a review of this literature see US Federal Trade Commission "Background Note" in *Application of Competition Policy to High Tech Markets*, (1997) Paris, OECD.
18 T Jorde & D Teece, *Antitrust, Innovation, and Competitiveness*, 1992, p 8.

tough in Germany because the FTA services broadcast more imported US material and films than in other countries in Europe. In *Bertelsmann/Kirch/Premiere* the Commission spent considerable time examining the relationship between FTA and pay TV re-affirming its previous conclusion but acknowledging that the wide availability and quality of FTA television (on average 30 channels) would affect the demand for pay TV. Interestingly, the Commission expressed concern that Bertelsmann and Kirch, which had significant interests in FTA, might co-ordinate to migrate programming over the pay TV. Some indicative evidence can be found from the take-up of pay TV in the larger countries in Europe. Table 5 gives pay TV penetration (number of subscribers as a percentage of the number of TV homes) and number of national FTA channels for the United Kingdom, France, Germany and Italy in 1997. This shows an inverse correlation between the number of FTA channels and pay TV penetration rates although this is not strong. The extreme case is Germany where terrestrial and satellite networks distribute at least 28 national FTA channels, and which has negligible pay TV amd a struggling digital platform DFI. Italy also has low pay TV take-up with two operators – Telepiu's D+ (owned by Canal +) and STREAM, a cable operation owned by Telecom Italia. It, like Germany, faces a highly commercialised public (the state owned RAI network with three channels partly advertiser funded) and six private FTA networks, and hundreds of regional channels. The United Kingdom and France have less competitive FTA systems, which in the United Kingdom is heavily regulated by public service programming regulation. These two also have higher pay TV take-up.

|  | Pay TV | | National |
|---|---|---|---|
| Country | Subscribers '000s | Penetration | FTA Channels |
| UK (Oct 98) | 7,051 | 30.1% | 4 |
| France (1997) | 950 | 5.0% | 5 |
| Italy (Dec 98) | 1,120 | 6.0% | 9 |
| Germany (Oct 98) | 1,650 | 5.9% | 28 |

*Source: New Media Markets; European Audiovisual Observatory Statistical Yearbook 1998; and relevant European Pay-TV companies.*

*Table 5: FTA v Pay TV in Europe, 1998*

There is more rigorous evidence on the question from the United States. In proceedings prior to the enactment of the US Cable Act 1992, attention focused on whether broadcast television was a source of competition to cable TV. This was part of the review of the previous effective competition standard administered by the FCC, which required four FTA channels for a cable pay TV franchise to be regarded as competitive. Two studies undertaken in 1990 provide evidence of the competitive relationship between broadcast and pay TV in the United States. Dertouzos and Wildman[19], and Crandall[20] found that cable networks in the United States facing competition from five or more broadcast TV channels had fewer subscribers, carried more channels in the basic tier, and had a lower price per basic channel than cable networks facing fewer channels. A more recent study by Crandall and Furchtgott-Roth[21] using panel data for 1992 confirmed this finding but with one modification. To quote:

> "Our model revealed that the demand for cable services is sensitive to the number of broadcast channels available to households without cable service... As the number of competing channels increases, demand for each type of cable service decreases. We found that the competitive effect of broadcast signals continues for all number of signals."[22]

No doubt these studies have problems and can be criticised. Nonetheless where the issue has been examined with some rigour it has been found that pay and FTA television compete, and that the effect is significant.

## 3. Network competition

Pay TV lies at the intersection of developments in television and telecommunications sectors. As a result it is increasingly seen as part of the telecommunications sector. Moreover, pay TV has a particular significance since its revenue contribution is seen as an important component inducing entrants to build local broadband networks which

---

19 J N Dertouzos & S S Wildman "Competitive effects of broadcast signals on cable", submitted as an attachment to the Comments of the National Cable Television Association in FCC Mass Media Docket 89-600, 1 March 1990.
20 R Crandall, "Regulation, competition, and cable performance" appended to TCI's reply Comments in FCC Mass Media Docket 90-04, 1990.
21 R W Crandall & Harold Furchtgott-Roth, *Cable TV – Regulation or Competition?* (1996) Washington DC: the Brookings Institution.
22 *Ibid*, at 146-147.

would provide real competition to dominant telecommunications operators. However, the dynamics of network competition, or between different platforms for pay TV, are not yet full understood. For example, experience has shown that outright competition between two or more pay TV operators using different (incompatible) platforms has often resulted in near financial collapse, due to inflated costs, low take-up, and the eventual merger or rationalisation of the sector. This has led some to believe that the industry may only be able to sustain one platform for each technology. A range of competitive issues are thus raised related to access, unbundling, CAS and other alleged gateways (see next section).

### Regulation of cable ownership

In many countries regulators and government have actively sought to encourage direct competition between different and identical network technologies. This has often led to the use of asymmetric regulation to restrict the activities of incumbent telecommunications operators. In particular, broadband cable is seen as offering direct competition to the local networks of established telecommunications operators, albeit on the back of the pay TV subscriber. It is therefore not surprising that the EC Commission has been concerned by the high level of ownership and operation of cable networks by dominant national telecommunications operators in Europe, particularly in Germany, the Nordic countries and Ireland.

The Commission has emphasised the potential role of "alternative infrastructures", particularly cable networks, in addressing the slow pace of innovation and delayed rollout of liberalised services in the EU.[23] Studies for the Commission have shown that EU tariffs were higher because of the lack of competing infrastructure, which in turn was inhibiting the development of new and innovative services placing the EU at a competitive disadvantage.[24] The OECD in a review of liberalised telecommunications markets (UK, USA, Sweden, Japan, Australia) found

23 "The impact of liberalisation of alternative terrestrial infrastructure for non-reserve services" (1994) Coopers & Lybrand; "The effects of liberalisation of satellite infrastructure on the corporate and closed user group market (1993) Analysis: "L'impact de l'authorisation de la fourniture de services de télécommunications liberalisés par les cablo-opérateurs" (1994) IDATE: "Future policy for telecommunications infrastructure and CATV networks – a path towards infrastructure liberalisation" (1994) Mercer Management Consulting.
24 Green Paper on the Liberalisation of Telecommunications Infrastructure and Cable Television Networks, EC Commission October 1994.

that network competition brings substantial benefits in the form of increased choice, greater innovation, better services, and greater investment in and modernisation of the telecommunication infrastructure.[25] The Commission has argued that dominant telecommunications' operators which own both cable TV and telecommunications networks have no incentive to attract users to the network which is the best suited for the provision of the relevant service, as long as they have spare capacity on the other network. On the contrary, in cases, where the provision of telecommunications network services is exclusive to the telecommunications operator, it has an incentive to raise its carriage fees in order to increase traffic on its other telecommunications network.[26] In Germany, and even in Southern Europe where there are few cable networks, there is a concern that PTOs will leverage their market power into a potentially competitive sector and even into content *e.g.* Telecom Italia in Italy and Telefonica Espania in Spain.

One response to these concerns is to ban the established dominant telecommunications operator from owning broadband cable networks, and delivering or owning video content. Within Europe, the United Kingdom has the longest history of this type of asymmetric regulation. Under the Telecommunications Act 1984 British Telecom was prohibited from delivering video services on its network, and was required to compete on an equal footing with others for new regional broadband cable network franchises. In the event it secured very few of these cable franchises with the result that regional cable networks were built by other operators mainly North American telcos. The United States also pursued a policy of asymmetric regulation designed to encourage the development of independent cable networks. The so-called Local Exchange Carriers (LECs) were prohibited from participation in cable networks in their service areas until 1994. The ban arose as a response to access disputes between cable networks and LECs.[27]

However, both these policies had mixed effects and did not encourage infrastructure competition. In the United Kingdom, far from

---

25 "Telecommunications infrastructure – the benefits of competition" (1995) Paris: OECD.
26 Dir 95/51.
27 For an excellent overview of the US position see L L Johnson *Toward Competition in Cable Television* (1994) Washington DC: American Enterprise Institute. Note that the competitive concern in the US has swung in the other direction with a view that cable networks have gained significant market power and therefore there is a need to foster network competition. The Telecommunications Act 1996 has liberalised LEC entry into video distribution.

the development of cable accelerating, it was stillborn, and after a decade had not become a serious challenge either to BT or a significant delivery platform for pay TV. In the United States, asymmetric regulation resulted in cable becoming the dominant means of delivering pay TV to 64% of TV homes, but with no significant competition, the cable operators acquired a monopoly position with perennial concerns that they have "hiked" basic cable subscriptions. The US Telecommunications Act 1996 seeks to remedy this situation by allowing LECs to enter pay TV.

In Australia a different approach was adopted. There Telstra, the national, (then) fully state-owned telecommunications' operator, was permitted to build and operate its own broadband network, and supply video services. This was part of a fixed duopoly policy which encouraged CW Optus to enter the local network and pay TV sectors. This, to European eyes, would appear almost to guarantee that competition was stillborn. However, rather surprisingly it led to intense rivalry between Telstra and Optus in the construction of broadband networks which now pass most homes in metropolitan Australia, with 80% to 90% "overbuild" in the main capital cities. However, while competition has been created, both operators are nursing substantial losses in respect of both network and pay TV operations, and a serious debate is taking place as to whether competition has been bought at the price of wasteful duplications of infrastructure.[28]

As a result of the above concerns, the EC Commission has taken action on a number of fronts as part of its liberalisation programme in the telecommunications sector. Directives designed to liberalise "alternative infrastructures" such as cable and the networks of utility industries, to compete directly with the dominant telecommunications' operators in the provision of telecommunications services.[29] The EC Commission *Cable Review* undertook an assessment of the impact of the joint provision of telecommunications and cable networks, and existing restrictions for the provision of cable television capacity over

---

28 For a detailed analysis of the Australian pay TV sector and competition law see C G
  Veljanovski "Pay TV in Australia – competition, consolidation and regulation", forthcoming.
29 The requirements to progressively open the telecommunications markets in the EU to 1 January
  1998 are set out in Dir 90/388/EEC of 28 June 1990 on competition in the markets for
  telecommunications services, as amended by Dir 94/46/EC of 13 October 1994, satellite
  communications, Dir 95/51/EC of 18 October 1995, abolition of restrictions on the use of cable
  television networks for the provision of already liberalised telecommunications services, Dir
  96/2/EC of 16 January 1996, mobile and personal communications, and Dir 96/19/EC of 13
  March 1996, full competition in telecommunications markets, OJ 1996 L74/13.

telecommunications network.[30] As a result it has proposed a draft Directive requiring the legal separation (in addition to the financial separation) of the cable operations of dominant telecommunications operator, thus falling far short of divestment.[31] The Commission has been active on other fronts. As already discussed it blocked digital alliances involving dominant telecommunications operators TOs in Germany, the Nordic countries, and was proceeding against Telefonica Espanas' proposed acquisition of cable network operator Sogecable in Spain. In July 1996 DG IV, under Article 86, began investigation of plans of three dominant operators, Telecom Italia, Telefonica Espana and (TE), to expand into cable television. In Ireland, Telecom Eireann increased its stake in the leading cable company from 60% to 75% and the company is considering using TE's telephone network to expand its broadcasting capacity.

## Economics of broadband competition

The central competitive issue is whether there is room for more than one broadband network. Or, put more formally, whether the economies of scale and scope are sufficient to lead to one platform, and as a result the competitive duplication of infrastructure, is uneconomic and wasteful. The economic efficiency of network competition is a matter, which has been relatively ignored. Under EC competition law there is not "efficiency defence" available to prospective "digital alliances" which pose a risk to competition. This is seen by some as a glaring gap, although it was omitted from the *Merger Regulation* to prevent the Commission reverting to old-style industrial policy in the administration of merger control policy.

The viability of direct competition in network provision depends on several supply and demand side considerations. The high construction costs of broadband cable networks places a limit on their number, especially since they require a variety of services to be commercially viable. These costs may be sufficiently high that the minimum scale justifies one network. However, given the existence of

---

30 Commission Communication concerning the review under competition rules of the joint provision of telecommunications and cable TV networks by a single operator and the abolition of restrictions on the provision of cable TV capacity over telecommunications networks, EC Commission 1998.

31 Draft Commission Directive amending Dir 90/388/EEC in order to ensure that telecommunications networks and cable TV networks owned by a single operator are separate legal entities, OJ 1998 C71/23.

an existing (upgradable) local network owned by the dominant telecommunication's operators, the financial considerations are finely balanced. Although costs and technology are constantly falling there is scepticism about the viability of interactive local broadband networks. For example, Dr Bruce Egan concluded after a detailed and exhaustive study of the economics of multimedia that:

> "Based on cost data ..., even under heroic assumptions of quick mass market deployment, the additional per household monthly revenues required to pay for the original investment is staggering ... Overall, the current demand and revenue data from the telecommunications sector indicate that a competitive service provider of two-way residential broadband network services face an uphill battle. New revenue growth is always going to be subject to the ability of households to afford to pay for fancy new services and the terminal devices that support them ... Even the teleco's own financial simulations for public broadband networks are pessimistic."[32]

The optimal and actual level of competition in network industries is also affected by *demand-side economies of scale* or so-called *network effects*. These exist when the number of other users affect the value of a product or service to a user.[33] As Professor Jean Tirole states:

> "Positive network externalities arise when a good is more valuable to a user the more users adopt the same good or compatible ones. The externality can be direct (a telephone user benefits from others being connected to the same network; computer software, if compatible, can be shared). It can also be indirect; because of increasing returns to scale in production, a greater number of complementary products can be supplied – and at a lower price – when the network grows (more programs are written for a popular computer; there are more video-cassettes compatible with a dominant video system; a popular automobile is serviced by more dealers)."[34]

It is therefore closely related to the economists' concept of an externality or third-party effect but arising not from technological or

32 B L Egan, *Information Superhighways Revisited – The Economics of Multimedia* (1996) Artech House.
33 C Shapiro & H R Varian *Information Rules – A Strategic Guide to the Network Economy* (1998) Harvard University Press, Case Associates "Misuse of network effects in competition cases recent applications to the computer industry" Casenote 6, January 1997.
34 J Tirole, *The Theory of Industrial Organization* (1989) MIT Press at 405.

cost factors but because the demand of consumers is interdependent.[35] It is argued that this demand interrelationship leads to reinforcing feedbacks that generate further growth and economies for larger networks. In the computer industry, for example, users will pay more for a popular computer system, other things being equal, or opt for a system with a larger installed base if the prices and other features of two competing systems are equivalent. This apparent advantage, it is argued, enables firms with a high market share to get larger, leading to monopolistic or at least oligopolistic market structures. The implication is that a small network is at a disadvantage to a large network, and that there may be a critical size for a network to be viable.[36]

The demand of individual subscribers to pay TV services does not exhibit such inter-dependency. The impact of an additional subscriber does not directly effect the value of pay TV to other subscribers. It is true that there are economies of density in cable networks as the average infrastructure costs, and the costs of settop boxes, decrease as total take-up increases. But this is a supply-side effect not unique to a specific cable operation but to the take-up of cable generally when unit costs fall with volume production.

However, where network effects will come into operation is when subscribers are required to choose between two or more technically incompatible pay TV platforms.[37] Prospective customers will recognise that if they purchase a satellite dish and settop decoder to receive the service from a pay TV operator, this cost may be sunk (unrecoverable) and that they may be locked because of the switching costs. This is particularly the case for satellite or off-air pay TV where satellite dishes cannot receive the signals of two different satellites, or if they broadcast on different technical standards. In these cases the ability of subscribers to switch between the services is limited by cost factors. In order to avoid being stranded potential subscribers may delay their purchase.

35 An externality is said to exist if a transaction imposes a cost or benefit on others not taken into account by the transacting parties. The classic case of an externality is pollution where the production of a good (for example, paint) gives rise to a third party effect (polluted rivers) not priced in the market. As a result the activity in question is over-expanded because society at large is effectively subsidising its production.

36 This concept was used by the Commission in *Worldcom/MCI* to force MCI to divert its internet backbone operation.

37 J Tirole, op cit, fn 34, Chap 10. B S Owen & S Wildman *Video Economics* (1996) Harvard University Press, Chap 7; S Besen & Saloner, "The economics of telecommunications standards" in W Crandall & K Flamm, eds, *Changing the Rules: Technological Change, International Competition, and Regulation in Communications*, (1989) Washington DC: American Enterprise Institute.

Often this is accompanied by strategic manoeuvres by the competing operators to increase customer confusion and denigrate its competitor's service. On the other hand, pay TV operators will often seek to deal with this problem by offering subsided reception equipment or renting it to subscribers.

This problem is compounded by exclusive programming. By splitting the most attractive programming, such as movies and sport, between two or more platforms, the value of any one pay TV package is reduced. Further, intense rivalry for such programme rights has usually lead to excessive prices, inflating the costs of the pay TV industry and affecting its commercial mobility.

Viewers switching costs have *ex-ante* and *ex-post* effects on competition.

(1) For the reasons discussed demand may be insufficient for only one operator. In the United Kingdom, during the late 1980s, two pay TV operators – Sky Television and British Satellite Broadcasting (BSB) - rushed to establish two different satellite pay TV platforms. These used different satellites, required the subscriber to purchase different settop boxes, and offered different programming. The presence of two incompatible systems was not at the time commercially viable, and the companies merged to form BSkyB which went on to become the success story of pay TV. Australia until recently had three separate platforms based on different technologies and exclusive content. The result has been continuing losses and the closure of the satellite based pay TV operator Australis.

(2) It is alleged to create an "aftermarket "problem. In *MSG Media Services* it was suggested that cable and satellite delivered pay TV were separate markets. The Commission expressly rejected the view of the parties that cable, satellite and terrestrial frequencies were regarded by consumers as interchangeable because there were differences between the three means of transmission "as far as the technical conditions and financing are concerned". The Commission was clear that cable and satellite do not form part of the same "relevant market":

> "While terrestrial transmission and satellite television only require the viewer to install an aerial or a satellite dish at his own expense, cable television presupposes the maintenance of a cable network financed by the viewer through cable fees. It makes a difference to the final consumers whether he has to incur a large amount of expenditure on a one-off basis for one form of transmission (for example, for the satellite

receiver) or whether he prefers to incur low-level, regular payments in the form of cable fees."[38]

The EC Commission further decided that cable and satellite were not interchangeable from the programme supplier's point of view given the differences in the costs involved.[39] This uses consumer switching cost to argue that if they are significant that *ex–post* the consumer is locked into a particular platform and therefore is potentially exploitable.

## 4. Conditional access

In the new world of competitive telecommunications the focus has shifted from the traditional concerns over natural monopoly regulation, to the control of "gateways". CAS is widely regarded as a "gateway" which can lead to competition problems. To quote *The Economist*:

> "This box is like a "gateway" between programme makers and viewers: whoever controls the box can decide which channels reach subscribers and which do not ... if there are only a few gateways – one encryption system, one local cable-TV firm – their owners have a degree of monopoly power. This is compounded by vertical integration: *i.e.* if gateway owners also make programmes. They may operate gateways not as toll gates, and thus allow any supplier through on payment of a fee, but as a portcullis, and bar and overcharge their competitors."[40]

The Commission has responded to pressure to regulate CAS on a number of fronts. The Digital Video Broadcasting Directive (DVB Directive)[41] sets out the framework for the regulation of conditional access, and other technical and non-technical services related to the provision of pay TV. In addition an essential facilities doctrine has been endorsed by the Commission. The Commission has been attracted to the doctrine for some time.[42] and while it has yet to be applied to pay

---

38 *Ibid* at para 41.
39 *Ibid* at para 42.
40 *The Economist*, 23 March 1996.
41 Dir 95/47/EC.
42 John Temple Lang, head of the telecommunications section of DG IV of the EC Commission, and a proponent of the essential facilities doctrine "The principle that companies in dominant positions have a legal duty to provide access to genuinely essential facilities on a non-discriminatory basis is one of great and increasing importance in telecommunications, transmission of energy, transport and many other industries. J Temple Lang, "Defining legitimate competition: companies' duties to supply competitors and access to essential facilities"(1994) 18 *Fordham International Law Journal* 437 at 524.

TV, the Commission's Access Notice[43] indicates that it will now be feature of regulation in the area. Indeed, DVB Directive and Access Notice are the mirror images of each other, one providing a system of *ex–ante* regulation, the other *ex–post* regulation of allegedly "bottleneck facilities".

The DVB Directive establishes a common transmission standard (MPEG2/DVB), deals with access, and the economic regulation of CAS. The Directive allows two approaches to be adopted by the pay TV industry – either a common interface (multicrypt) for settop boxes or access to a CAS on "fair, reasonable and non-discriminatory terms" (simulcrypt). In physical terms the a standard interface will involve plugging in different CA modules into the back of the set-top box using detachable PC-Cards or incorporate the same encryption system on its services using same or different smartcards which are slotted into the front of the box. It has thus shied away from a mandatory common technical standard advocated in particular by UK terrestrial broadcasters and politicians.

Article 4 of the DVB Directive imposes economic regulation on CAS operators. The tariffs for technical services must be "a fair reasonable and non-discriminatory". The UK implementation of the Directive breaks down the CAS supply chain into four elements.[44] – *technical services* – subscriber management services (SMS), subscriber authorisation services (SAS), and encryption services (ES); and *non-technical services* – customer management services (CMS). Technical Services are subject to the full force of the DVB Directive; namely, the requirement to supply services on a fair, reasonable and non-discriminatory basis. To ensure that these aims are met, separate accounts are required. *Non-technical services,* on the other hand, are only required to keep separate accounts.

---

43 Notice on the application of competition rules to access agreements in the telecommunications sector framework, relevant markets and principles, OJ 1998 C265. K Coates, "Commission Notice on the application of the competition rules to access agreements in the telecommunications sector", *Competition Policy Newsletter*, 1998/2, DG IV European Commission. H Ungerer "Ensuring efficient access to bottleneck network facilities: the case of telecommunications in the European Union" Competition Seminar, Florence, 13 November 1998. http//eropa.ue.int/comm/dg04/speech/eight/en/sp98056.

44 Proposals for digital terrestrial digital terrestrial television – the Government proposals, August 1995, enacted as The Advance Television Services Regulations 1996 (SI 1996 No 3151) and The Regulation of Conditional Access for Digital Television Services – OFTEL Guidelines, 1997.

The essential facility doctrine is a species of refusal to supply with a chequered and controversial application. It was originally developed in cases involving railways in the US. The railway company owns the track and most of the rolling stock providing freight services. The track is regarded as an essential facility – some asset or service which is essential for others to effectively compete in the freight sector. The railway company can block competition to its freight business by preventing use of its tracks and/or charging high fees to other freight companies. This railway model has been extended to the communications industry in the US although its application in EC law to date has been limited.[45]

Although the law is unclear the principal competitive concern arises over the potential for vertical foreclosure. It would seem that strict application would require:

(a) a 100% monopoly of the facility or, it is argued, prohibitive costs of constructing a duplicate facility; and

(b) that the owner of the facility is vertically integrated and therefore in direct competition with other users.

Further, the essential facility doctrine does not imply mandatory common carriage or that the owner of the facility is entitled to earn a return to its investment in the facility.

## Economics of access

The DVB Directive is premised on the assumption that whoever controls CAS is the "gatekeeper" of the digital pay market, and can act monopolistically. If a pay channel wants to gain access to a delivery platform with a substantial installed subscriber base, to be denied

---

45 There have been a number of television cases which have been seen as the percusors of an essential facilities doctrine: *Magill/RTE/BBC* (Case T-69/89 *Radio Telefis Eireann* v *Commission*, Case T-70/89 *British Broadcasting Corporation Enterprises Ltd* v *Commission*) – a complex set of cases concerning the supply of programme listing information/schedule to downstream competitors by BBC and RTE. Held: refusal to supply anti-competitive. Case 311/84 *Télémarketing (Télémarketing (CBEM) SA* v *Compagnie Luxembourgeoise de Télédiffusion SA and Information Publicité Benelux SA* –– a television station with a monopoly of commercial airtime makes advertising time available only to advertisers who also use the phone lines and telephonists of a phone-in marketing company associated with the station. Held: refusal to supply an abuse under Article 86. Case C-7/97 *Oscar Bronner* v *Mediaprint* – refusal of a media undertaking housing a dominant position in one EU Member State to include a daily rival newspaper of another undertaking in the same Member State in its newspaper home-delivery scheme – see especially Advocate General Jacobs' opinion.

access, or offered expensive access, would act as a short-term inhibition to entry. However, for this to have real competitive consequences it must also be shown that the costs of establishing a separate CAS operation on the same delivery systems was prohibitively expensive, in the sense that one CAS serving the entire market is cheaper than two or more serving parts of the market, *i.e.* CAS is to be considered a natural monopoly activity.

In reality the CAS market is competitive. There are a number of CAS systems competing world-wide for business. It is also the case that different CAS systems coexist in the same market on different delivery platforms for analogue pay TV – cable, satellite, DTT, MVDS, SMATV etc. In the United Kingdom different encryption systems exist for cable and satellite delivery, and for digital cable, DTT and BSkyB. Furthermore, these can and will be integrated over time by the use of "sidecars" (which enable dual encryption), translators and other technical innovations. The Internet and the development of intelligent TV sets which are addressable will eventually deal automatically with different encryption systems just in the same way as a computer can, or TV sets which have the ability to deal with PAL, SECAM and NICAM standards. It should also be recognised that there is nothing wrong with technical incompatibilities *per se* – they reflect the rivalry between different manufacturers in the market place backed by their willingness to invest risk capital to establish new businesses!

It is also difficult to characterise CAS or settop boxes as a "gateway" for another reason. A CAS operator who is not active in other parts of the pay TV industry has no incentive to favour one party over another, or to limit utilisation of its CAS. It would seek to maximise the return to the provision of CAS services by selling to as many channels/services as possible. Moreover, open access to CAS does not guarantee access to delivery networks (cable, terrestrial off-air, and/or satellite networks). This requires a separate delivery contract/lease usually with a separate entity. Article 4 of the DVB Directive does not imply common carrier or mandatory access to carriage, nor does the essential facility doctrine.

It is only when the CAS operator is *vertically integrated* with pay TV services that a potential problem arises. A vertically integrated CAS operator has a potential conflict of interest since it supplies a service (CAS) to its competitors. In these circumstances it may use CAS to restrict competition by denying access or imposing unfavourable terms. Some economists have called this tactic *raising rivals' costs*. The vertically integrated firm can "price squeeze" its non-integrated buyers by raising its price above competitive levels. Such foreclosure is a recurring problem in the communications sector *e.g.* a local telephone company uses dominance in transmission (primary market) to leverage its market power in a secondary market such as customer premises equipment. However, the use of a CAS operator to extract monopoly profits from programming is dubious. This is hotly rejected by many economists. Their view is that it is not profitable to leverage market power in one market to another market in the vertical chain. If CAS is the source of monopoly then "there is only one monopoly profit". The owner of an encryption system which is a monopoly can extract whatever monopoly profits exist through pricing encryption service and the vertical integration will not improve its profits.

Another concern is that existing analogue pay TV/CAS operators (BSkyB, Kinnevik, Nethold, Kirch, Canal Plus, and Telepiú) have first-mover advantages and an installed subscriber base which can be leveraged to transfer their dominance in analogue to digital pay TV. The existence of a large installed subscriber base of analogue subscribers has conflicting pulls on the operators' reaction to digital TV. Digital TV undermines and threatens the position of successful analogue pay TV operations since it enables the entry of competitors, thus leading to writing off the potential returns on its investment in analogue, and requires considerable costs in re-engineering technology and programming for a digital service. Also, because for many years it will be serving both analogue and digital subscribers, there will be a duplication of costs. The second, and related factor, is that digital TV will require new decoders, antennas and televisions. Thus, for the established pay TV operators this will require beginning from scratch and the return to a new digital subscriber will be worth less because the likelihood is that they will come from their analogue service. Thus, all things being equal, an analogue pay TV operator would be inclined to suppress the development of digital or delay its introduction. On the other hand, if the introduction of digital looks inevitable the analogue operator will act to secure its position rapidly. It will have an incentive to deter entry and to deploy its preferred CAS system. One cannot, therefore, overlook the possibility that existing analogue pay TV/CAS operators will act strategically if credible entrants in the digital pay TV sector emerge. This may take the form of the strategic use of misleading or exaggerated pre-announcement designed to deter competitors from establishing.

The DVB Directive and the essential facilities doctrine both recognise that the parties who have created and built an infrastructure should be permitted to earn a return on their investment. The attempt through regulation to contain the size and profits of pay TV/CAS operators may have a deleterious effect. It substitutes regulation for the competitive process. Few would dispute that penicillin is better than leeches in curing disease. But if in order to get penicillin one must tolerate temporary monopoly then public policy needs to take this aspect of the innovative process into its regulatory framework. Why condemn a temporary monopoly of penicillin if penicillin saves many more lives than the competitive supply of leeches? Why condemn monopoly if the lure of excess profits leads others to search for newer and better drugs to displace penicillin? Regulation should be concerned not with whether innovative firms have shared fairly the market spoils with their less innovative rivals, but whether genuine market power exists: in other words, an *ex–ante* rather than *ex–post* view of competition.

The trend of increasing regulation is also dangerous in this regard. It creates free riders and opportunists who reduce the incentive to innovate. Many potential participants will recognise that they can gain when others create a new market by simply asserting essential facilities and gaining cheap access. The potential investor in CAS will recognise the strategic use of law in this way will reduce his return, and this will encourage adaptive responses that are costly (such as filling capacity with channels) or reducing or avoiding investment in CAS/digital television. The UK Government, for example, rejected a mandatory common interface because

" ... such a move could discourage early investment in decoder development and production; second movers could free ride on first movers' investment."

## Economics of standard setting

The alternative to access regulation is a mandatory common standard imposed on the pay TV industry. This has so far been resisted. Nonetheless, the idea that markets cannot be trusted to set efficient standards is a prevalent and powerful one.

The discussion above of network effect is applicable to the analysis of standards. Economic literature points to potential market failures in the selection of technical standards. It identifies circumstances where the wrong technical standard may be selected. The literature refers to *excess inertia* arising from the fear of early adopters of a new technology, namely the risk of losing initial investment because the technology is not adopted by a sufficiently large portion of the market. In this case the parties' fears of being "stranded" with a low-value technology[46] may result in deferring its adoption. If many in the market take this stance there is "excess inertia" resulting in an efficient standard not being adopted, even though buyers would be better off if it were. Others have questioned this conclusion, arguing that this literature offers a set of hypothetical market failures, misinterprets the limited evidence, and that market forces do in practice lead to better choices than governments.[47] It does, however, formalise some common sense concerns about the development of industry standards and the implicit assumptions which underlie the fear of potential market failure.

While one cannot rule out the possibility of market inefficiency, one equally cannot assume that government participation in the standard setting process will be better. There is little hard evidence that markets do fail in setting technical standards and there are examples within the pay TV area that government has generated considerable inefficiency in seeking to foster preferred standards. Just as there can be market failures there can be Government failure. In practice, government policy–makers lack the expertise to set ideal standards at just the right moment. As a result, government policy in standard setting can be more anti than pro-competitive.

In the European pay TV sector the classic case of administrative failure was DBS and D-MAC. Here the international and European Community decided on a technology and a structure for the introduction of satellite television which was excessively expensive and over–engineered relative to market conditions. The WARC-77 agreement to use high-powered satellites was confined as far as possible to national territories. This attempt to minimise so-called "overspill" was impractical and expensive and pandered to national political concerns rather than commercial reality. The attempt to force the emerging satellite industry to use the D2-MAC standard when there was a major installed base of PAL receivers heaped unnecessary costs on an already high-risk investment.

The HDTV technology aroused much excitement in the early 1990s. This technology would allow cinema quality pictures in the home.

---

46 J Farrell & G Saloner, "Standardization, compatibility and innovation", (1985) 16 *RAND Journal of Economics* 70-83; S Besen & L Johnson, *Compatibility Standards, Competition, and Innovation in the Broadcasting Industry* (1986) RAND Publication No R-3453-NSF.
47 S Liebowitz & H Margolis, "The fable of the keys" (1990) 33 *Journal of Law & Economics* 1.

However, HDTV required significantly more information to be transmitted than conventional television. Given the constraints on bandwidth, much of the HDTV technology centred on the development of compression techniques. As a consequence, entirely new equipment for both sending and receiving HDTV transmissions was needed. Moving to HDTV required not only the development of new television sets but also that entertainment has to be recorded in a new format and transmitted to new satellite via new dishes and new tuners. Since HDTV required the co-ordination of many different industries, governments believed that they had a role to play in establishing a common standard. The EC mistakenly supported an analogue-based technology based on the MAC standard. In 1986, the EC issued a Directive requiring medium and high-powered satellite broadcasters to use the MAC standard. However, broadcasters undermined this move, notably Sky TV, circumventing the directive by continuing to use the PAL standard transmitting from low-powered satellites.

In 1991, the EC adopted a further Directive which required that after 1996 services must be able to be broadcast simultaneously (in both conventional and MAC format). New TV sets thus had to be fitted with a MAC decoder. Despite this new Directive, the advisability of the MAC standard began to be questioned by April 1992. In addition to concerns over the need for further large investments, EC officials became concerned about the progress made in the United States with digital HDTV – a far superior technology. By February 1993, the Commission finally admitted defeat and announced that European HDTV would follow the digital standard similar to that being set by the United States.

## 5. Conclusion

A dynamic competitive process is at the heart of the evolution of digital television. Competition is a "discovery process" in which innovation is reducing barriers to entry; to quote Professor Joseph Schumpeter:

> "competition from the new commodity, the new technology, the new source of supply, the new organization ... competition which strikes at the margins of profits and the outputs of existing firms but at the foundations and their very lives."[47]

---

48 J Schumpeter, *Democracy, Capitalism and Socialism*.

Yet the regulatory approach appears to see the development of digital in fairly static structural terms, and to employ telecommunications-type regulation to deal with perceived problems. The discussion above suggests that this approach is misconceived and unduly rigid taking a narrow short-term view of what is essentially a longrun evolutionary process. It focuses on short-term price behaviour ignoring the real dynamic of digital pay TV, which is non-price competition. The use of asymmetric regulation, gateways and the essential facility doctrine substitute for detailed analysis of the competitive constraints on service and infrastructure providers. Finally, demand-side and supply-side economics of scale and scope in the development of infrastructure and pay TV platforms point again to a more complex competitive process which may limit efficient competition in the formative stages of development of pay TV.

Dr Cento Veljanovski

## Bibliography

"Market definitions in telecommunications", Case Research Paper No 1, December 1998

"Defining airline markets", Case Research Paper No 2, December 1998

"Competitive regulation of digital pay TV", Case Research Paper No 3, January 1999

"Pricing calls to mobiles', Case Research Paper No 4, January 1999

"EC competition policy in banking", Case Research Paper No 5, forthcoming.

# Exhausting all the Arguments: · A Short Guide to the · Economics of Trade Mark Exhaustion

## Cliff Stevenson

The author is Chief Economist at Rowe & Maw, 20 Black Friars Lane, London EC4V 6HD. Telephone (44-171) 248 4282; cstevenson@roweandmaw.co.uk. The author wishes to thank Jeremy Kempton for his helpful comments on this article.

*European Economics & Law*
Palladian Law Publishing Ltd

# Exhausting all the Arguments:
· A Short Guide to the ·
Economics of Trade Mark Exhaustion

## *1.* Introduction to a controversial issue

Since the *Silhouette* judgment[1] the issue of trade mark exhaustion has become a particularly controversial one in the European Community. The proponents of international exhaustion argue that the current regime allows trade mark holders to differentiate between markets in a way that is disadvantageous to European consumers. They argue that, as long as the first sale is a legitimate one, rights holders should not be allowed to segment their markets internationally so as to protect high prices. Evidence is often provided through price comparisons between the EC and the United States showing price differences of at least 50%. In these circumstances, so it is argued, there is no justification in the current system of Community exhaustion.

On the other side of the argument are the rights holders. While there is a general acceptance of Community exhaustion in the context of the single market, international exhaustion is perceived as an undesirable weakening of intellectual property rights. Trade mark holders point out that they have invested considerable sums of money in establishing their trade marks, for which they have a right to adequate intellectual property protection. At stake, they argue, are future investments and jobs in the EC.

The purpose of this article is to consider the economics of trade mark exhaustion. Before doing so, it is useful to consider the economic justification for trade marks.

---

1 Case C-355/96. This decision confirmed the rights of trade mark holders to prevent parallel imports from outside the EEA.

## 2. **The economic justification for trade marks**

At first glance, trade marks are a superficial concept. Two products can be 100% identical but vary considerably in their desirability to consumers because one has the label of a fashionable brand while the other has nothing but a "Made in China" label.

In certain situations it is clear that trade marks are about fashion statements. An article of clothing can retail at a higher price if it has a brand label than if it does not. One reason for this is that the consumer enjoys any "prestige" that may arise from wearing the article. Whether the prestige comes from factors such as exclusivity or status amongst peers, it most likely occurs because there has been some investment in the brand name.

The trade mark is, therefore, the signal/confirmation of this prestige. To the extent that companies invest in creating a brand image, there is an economic justification in protecting this investment. If trade marks could not be registered, no-one would invest in brand image (as the brand could immediately be copied) and thus consumers who enjoy the prestige of such products would lose out. Thus, economic welfare would be reduced.

However, brands are not just about image and prestige. There is an additional and more important role that they play for consumers by signalling the quality that can be expected of the product. If consumers do not have reliable indicators of quality, markets will fail to operate efficiently. We can see this in a simplified example.

Take a situation where there are 10 companies manufacturing men's suits. Each of the 10 companies produces a different quality of suit ranging from very low to very high quality. If all the suits are the same colour and made of similar material, the only way of differentiating them is the brand name.

If there is no brand name on any of the suits, what would happen? Consumers would be taking a chance when they bought a high price suit, in that they would not know whether they were buying a low or high quality suit. In this situation, nobody would pay a high price for the suit. Consumers would prefer to buy lower price suits where the expectation is that they may be buying a low quality suit. There is no risk that the suit will be overpriced. The economic problem in such a situation is that, if there was no form of differentiating the product in advance of purchasing and using it, the high quality suits would not be able to command a higher price.

This is a classic case of market failure. The higher quality producers (who presumably incur greater production costs) cannot realise a sufficient price to cover their additional costs and therefore they will stop producing the higher quality product. Thus, only lower quality products remain on the market.

Trade marks provide a method of correcting this market failure. In principle, a brand name is only a meaningful concept if it has been created (probably through significant investment). Advertising, pre-sales and after-sales service, and consumer guarantees are some of the means by which brand images are created and reinforced. In theory, investment in such factors is only worthwhile if the product is of high quality. This, therefore, is the principal means by which consumers are informed of the quality of a product in advance of purchasing it. A high quality good can therefore be priced higher than a low quality good, because the consumer is able to have confidence in the quality.

Understanding brand creation, marketing and consumer behaviour is not an exact science. Some brands may be able to create and sustain an image of high quality but actually not live up to the image. On the other hand, perceived low quality brands may in fact be as good as high quality brands. Nevertheless, over time, as long as the market is a competitive one, brand investment will only be viable if the products live up to consumer expectations. Advertising and other brand investment expenditure can only be recovered in the long term if the product meets the standard expected of the brand.

Trade mark protection is crucial to this market–correcting mechanism to ensure that market failure is avoided. Without trade mark protection, imitations of the product could free-ride on the brand investment. The investor must have the exclusive right to use the trade mark to ensure that there is an incentive to produce high quality products.

The above economic justification of trade marks is relatively well accepted and not in itself controversial. The debate on international exhaustion does not call into question the right to protect trade marks. The issue relates to the moment in time when that right is exhausted.

## 3. Why does the parallel import issue arise?

Parallel trade can occur in any situation where there are arbitrage opportunities created by differences in prices for the same product in different markets. Parallel trade can take place in many different ways. For example, a product that has been exported may be imported back into the domestic market (*i.e.* there is an import transaction parallel to the original export). This was the situation in *Silhouette* where Austrian sunglasses exported to Bulgaria at low prices were brought back and sold in the Austrian market. Alternatively, it may be that exports from country 1 to country 2 are diverted to country 3, and thus compete with direct exports from country 1 to country 3.

Opportunities for parallel importing can only arise when producers are able to price on a different basis in different markets. The parallel importer is interested in buying goods in low priced markets and re-selling them in high price markets. By definition, this implies that markets are segmented and producers are able to price discriminate between the various markets.

An important question to consider is whether price discrimination *per se* is a bad thing? Is it necessarily harmful that different prices are charged in different markets? When some form of price discrimination can take place, there may be strong commercial reasons to offer lower prices to certain groups while the group in question clearly gains from lower prices (*i.e.* both producers and consumers gain). If the price in the high price market is based on a normal profit made on cost of production, the low price market may represent a price with no profit or even below cost. In such circumstances, it is possible that price discrimination increases economic welfare.

Nevertheless, this is not to say that all price discrimination is good. There may be a problem in the situation where monopoly profits are obtained in one market while a normal profit is received in another market. In such a situation, inadequate competition is allowing monopoly profits to be made in the first market. The fact that the markets are segmented allows the monopoly profits to remain unchallenged. Allowing products from the low priced market to be supplied to the high priced market would ensure that greater competition existed and the monopoly profits were removed. In such a case, preventing price discrimination would increase economic welfare.

It is therefore clear that, if there is a parallel importing opportunity, there must be some form of price discrimination. It is also apparent that, depending on the circumstances with regard to competition, it may or may not be desirable to allow parallel imports.

A key issue is the extent to which trade mark protection is the basis by which markets are segmented? Do trade marks create a situation in which price discrimination can take place? Is it possible that allowing companies to prevent parallel imports of products on the grounds of trade mark permits these companies to take part in unfair price discrimination? These are the fundamental questions of this article.

## 4. A ban on parallel imports is different to a ban on imports: the former is only a problem if there is a competition issue

Some supporters of international exhaustion consider the ban on parallel imports of trade marked products from outside the EEA to be protectionist. Such people talk of a ban on parallel imports as if it is equivalent to a ban or a quota on all imports of the product in question.

However, it should be noted that a ban on parallel imports only restricts importation of products bearing the same trade mark. It does not prevent importation of very similar products bearing different trade marks.

The difference is clear. An import ban clearly reduces competition. Whether a ban on parallel imports reduces competition depends on the extent to which competition exists in the first place. If there is one global producer of a product, a ban on parallel imports is bad for competition as it allows the global monopolist to discriminate between markets in a way that may work to the disadvantage of consumers (the restriction in intra-brand competition allows the monopolist to further exploit his position). If there are many producers of similar products under different brand names (*i.e.* strong inter-brand competition), actual and/or potential, any exploitation of consumers in the high priced market would not be sustainable due to competition between the brands. That is, if one brand is sold at profits in excess of a normal profit after taking into account the brand investment costs, other brands would be able to undercut the excessively priced brand while still making a normal profit.

Thus, the level of competition is crucial to the issue of whether restricting parallel imports on the grounds of trade marks permits unfair price discrimination to occur.

## 5. The existence of price differences does not mean that international exhaustion brings automatic gains for consumers

If there is not sufficient inter-brand competition, producers may be able to exploit consumers in the Community market with high prices while selling cheaper in certain countries outside the EEA. In such a circumstance, the ban on parallel imports allows the producers to maintain this position. Allowing parallel imports would undermine this and, therefore, may bring a gain for consumers.

However, it is not clear that gains for consumers would be automatic.

First, there can be many reasons for price differences unrelated to trade mark protection. Factors that may affect the price comparison are the conditions surrounding the sale (*e.g.* quantity, discounts available, credit terms *etc*), sales taxes and changes in exchange rates. For these reasons, apparent price differences can be significantly reduced when all appropriate adjustments are made.

Secondly, all the gains from parallel imports will not necessarily be passed onto consumers. If the problem is a lack of competition in the domestic market, parallel importers may buy in low price markets and re-sell at prices only just undercutting the high domestic prices. That is, they may make more profit rather than passing lower prices to consumers.

A third point is that parallel importers may have no commitment towards supplying the product on a long term basis. Discount retailers can make news headlines by offering one line of a brand name product at discount prices for a limited period. However, it may have no commitment either in terms of providing a source of long term supply or of supplying a range of products.

A further point is that products that appear to be the same may not be identical. For example, brand name soft drinks can vary considerably in taste according to the country in which it is sold. Likewise a brand name car fuel may have different composition in cold countries than that in hot countries. Thus, consumer confusion may be created as a result of parallel imports (thus undermining one of the main economic justifications of parallel imports).

As a result of the latter point, it can be seen that international exhaustion inevitably implies a globalisation of branding. Currently, the same brand name may be used for slightly different products in different countries. In order for the concept of trade marks not to be undermined, it would be necessary in many cases to create global brands. Brands would have to be created equally in all markets. This would involve similar levels of investment, otherwise the free-rider problem occurs. Thus, the uniqueness of particular products in particular markets may be lost which may work to the disadvantage of consumers.

An additional point is that international exhaustion is definitely undesirable if it results in increased piracy. One advantage of the ban on parallel imports is that imports, *per se*, are banned and therefore there is no need to prove that they are counterfeit. For branded products, piracy is a major problem and, for certain products, allowing parallel imports may open the floodgates for counterfeit products. This would clearly be detrimental to producers (whose investment is undermined) and consumers (who are not receiving the product they think they are buying.

Many people believe that the problem of piracy should be dealt with through better enforcement of intellectual property rights. This is clearly the "first-choice" solution. However, while the resources for such enforcement are not in place, and the sophistication of pirating techniques increases, the benefit of better protection against piracy, even if not an end in itself, may well be considered to be a significant benefit of the ban on parallel imports.

## 6. Conclusion

Many critics of the current exhaustion regime compare the ban on parallel imports to an import ban and make the conclusion that introducing international exhaustion must be desirable.

It is the argument in this article that there are circumstances in which introducing international exhaustion may not be desirable, either for trade mark holders or consumers. In making the judgement on whether international exhaustion would be desirable, it should be remembered that there are good arguments on each side of the debate. It is likely that the conclusions would differ for different sectors or markets.

There are many cases where the ban on parallel imports allows price discrimination that improves economic welfare (*i.e.* where the high priced market is a competitive one). In such a situation, by not allowing parallel imports, producers are free to make additional export sales the basis of prices based on marginal costs. However, such prices would not be viable across domestic and export sales and, therefore, international exhaustion would harm producers in this case.

The most problematic situation identified in this article is the one where there is a problem with the level of competition. That is, where the price in the domestic market is high because there is insufficient competition and the export price is the normal, competitive price. In this case, although allowing parallel imports may treat the malady, it is not the cure. In fact, it may well increase the harm to the economy as the position of trade mark holders is undermined.

Cliff Stevenson

# Opening up the Market for Postal Services

### Peter Scott

The author is a director of the economics consultants, MMD Ltd, 78-80 St John Street, London EC1M 4HR. Telephone: (44-171) 251 3925.

*European Economics & Law*

Palladian Law Publishing Ltd

# Opening up the Market for Postal Services

## 1. Introduction

The single market has been a while in coming in the utilities sector. In postal services, the first sign of its approach was the Green Paper published by the European Commission in 1992 on the development of the Single Market for postal services. Discussion of the ideas in this document proceeded at a leisurely pace over five years, while the market moved on and some Member States pressed ahead with liberalisation. At the end of 1997 Directive 97/67/EC finally appeared, setting out a new framework for postal services.

This article describes the main features of that Directive and discusses the various studies set in motion by the European Commission in the light of it, as aids in preparing new proposals for further liberalisation which the Commission is now due to produce.

## 2. The Directive

The principal elements of the Directive are:

- an obligation on each Member State to guarantee the maintenance of a universal postal service across its whole territory (Articles 3, 4);
- a limit on the price or weight of items of mail which Member States may reserve to their national Post Office (Article 7);
- obligations on each Member State in respect of the price and quality of the universal service in its territory (Articles 6, 12, 16-20);
- an obligation on each Member State to designate a regulatory authority for postal services which is legally and operationally separate from the postal operator(s) (Article 22);
- the prospect of further moves to open up the market to competition, following a review of the sector and proposals from the European Commission (Article 7).

## 3. **Universal service**

### Definition

Universal service is defined in the Directive (Article 4) as the collection and delivery of letters, domestic parcels up to 10kg in weight and cross-border parcels up to 20kg in weight once each weekday. Member States may increase the domestic weight limit to 20kg. Delivery is to every address in the national territory, with rare exceptions for remote areas. Collection is from a network of collection points accessible to people everywhere in the national territory. The universal service also includes services for registered and insured postal items.

### Cost

A difficulty with the imposition of a universal service relates to its cost. Clearly it has a cost, but no one is sure what it is, nor how it should be calculated. Opinions differ on how to set about calculating it. One of the studies commissioned by Directorate-General XIII as part of the promised review of the sector by the European Commission has examined the issues in this area. National Economic Research Associates (NERA) reported in October 1998 on the "Costing and financing of universal services in the postal sector in the European Union".

There are two main views on how to estimate the cost of the universal service. One is to look at postal flows in detail: in principle at each origin-destination flow, although in practice only much more aggregated flows can be considered. The point is to try to work out which flows a postal operator would not carry, at present prices, if it did not have to, and how much better off it would be if it stopped carrying the ones it loses money on.

This is not a straightforward exercise in any of its elements. National postal operators ("Post Offices") rarely keep, and even more rarely disclose, information on the profitability of individual groups or classes of route. One illustration of the complexity, and the need for judgement as well as measurement, is that providing a universal service has commercial value to a postal operator. The loss of part of that value has to be set against the gain of dropping an individually unprofitable route or set of routes.

The other main contender, as a way of estimating the cost of providing the universal service, is to look at how much profit the Post Office in each Member State is likely to lose if competitors are allowed into its business. The assumption here is that each Post Office is currently receiving an acceptable level of subsidy, or making an acceptable level of profit (Member States differ in whether their Post Offices make or lose money). So any profit foregone by introducing competition will have to be replaced if the Post Office is to continue to provide what it now does with an acceptable rate of return.

This approach also requires a complex set of estimates and judgements. How much business would competitors win, under what conditions and at what prices? How far would the Post Office have to reduce its prices to sustain an acceptable share of the market? How big a share is that? Since the national Post Office in all Member States is now a monopoly, or near monopoly, how can we judge how efficient it is, and thus how much of the profit it may lose to competitors is a real cost of the universal service which needs to be replaced?

The NERA study opts for the first of these approaches. It presents estimates, for each Member State, of the cost of those elements of the universal service which Post Offices would not run at present prices if they were not required to do so. The definition of universal service used in this study is wider than the one in the Directive and is not harmonised. It is the definition currently in use in each Member State and this varies quite widely. Some, for example, require Saturday deliveries of letters and parcels. Others require Saturday delivery only of newspapers. Others have no Saturday deliveries.

This study presents estimates for the cost of the universal service obligation in two ways. One is on a fully-distributed cost basis. That is, all costs incurred by the Post Office, including overheads that do not directly relate to collection, sorting, transport or delivery, are included in the calculation of an average cost of handling unprofitable mail. On that basis the cost of the universal service is estimated to be around 5% of postal revenues, with some variation by Member State, from a low of 0.7% to a high of 14.3%. These are not large proportions, but they compare with an average profit margin for national Post Offices across the European Union of some 3% in 1997.

The other way in which NERA[1] present the figures, and the one they consider the most appropriate method of calculation, is to show the net avoided cost of the universal service. That is, this method takes account only of those costs which would not be incurred as a direct result of ceasing to handle the mail in question – leaving unallocatable overheads

---

1  NERA, "Costing & financing of universal services in the postal sector in the European Union" (October 1998), Table 5.2, p 64.

intact. On that, preferred basis, NERA's estimates of the cost of the universal service are much lower, indeed at or close to zero for most Member States.

## Financing

If the universal service has an agreed cost, there are two main ways of funding it which have been suggested in the European debate on postal services so far. The first is the traditional way: give the national Post Office a monopoly, so that it can use monopoly profits to cross-subsidise loss-making parts of the universal service. The Directive currently allows Member States, if they so choose, to reserve certain postal services to a single operator so as to let it cross-subsidise the universal service in this way.

The "reservable" area of postal services is limited in the Directive in two ways. First, postal services may only be reserved "to the extent necessary to ensure the maintenance of a universal service". Thus, presumably, if no detectable cost can be agreed then no reservation is permitted. Second, the Directive limits the kinds of mail which can be reserved. Reservable kinds are ordinary domestic letters costing less than five times the basic letter price or weighing less than 350g together with, for the time being, direct mail and cross-border mail within those price/weight thresholds. Other services (like parcels, newspapers, unaddressed mail, mail items weighing more than 350g) may not be reserved after February 1999.

For some Member States the introduction of these new rules represents more of a change than for others. In France, for example, the carriage of all items of mail up to 2kg has hitherto been a monopoly of the French Post Office. Sweden and Finland do not formally reserve any mail flows. Germany cut the limit for ordinary domestic mail to 200g, and for direct mail to 50g, in 1998. For the United Kingdom, not entirely by chance, 350g roughly corresponds with the price of £1, the existing threshold for the Post Office monopoly.

If any services are reserved to the national Post Office, then accounting separation between the reserved and non-reserved services is required (Article 14).

The other way of financing the universal service which is explicitly envisaged in the Directive is for a Member State to establish a compensation fund. A Member State can require contributions wherever it judges the financial burden of providing the universal service is unfair

(Article 9). Contributions to the fund may be required from anyone who is licensed to provide postal services, and payments may be made from the fund to the operator or operators who provide the universal service. In practice, this mechanism has been used in Finland in a way which has effectively deterred competitive entry into a market for postal services which has, in law, been wholly liberalised for years.

The Directive is silent on whether contributions to such a compensation fund out of government budgetary revenue will be treated as falling outside the state aids provisions of the EC Treaty. It is implicit that they will be, both because Member States are required to guarantee the provision of a universal service, and because the funding of the compensation fund from other postal operators is permissive, not compulsory. Post Offices in some Member States are robustly profitable at present. But several Member States have Post Offices which run deficits year after year. Only with liberalisation and the entry, or thwarted entry, of competitors, will state aid questions start to be raised in this field.

With the approach of liberalisation, there have been several well-publicised examples of purchase by state-owned national Post Offices of private postal operators in other Member States or elsewhere. The most dramatic have been the purchase by the (now privatised) Netherlands Post Office (TPG) of the international courier company TNT, and the purchase by the German Post Office (Deutsche Post AG) of a 25% stake in the international courier company, DHL, and more recently of the major international transport services company, Danzas. Questions are already being raised about how much public money is involved in such transactions, for example, in connection with the recent purchase by the UK's Royal Mail of a private parcel operator in Germany.

Compensation to the provider(s) of the universal service from the Fund is required by the Directive (Article 9) to be transparent, non-discriminatory and proportional to the financial burden of the universal service. The simplest way of showing that these conditions have been met is probably that envisaged in the new German postal law[2]. This is that the government should invite competitive tenders for the supply of any part of the universal service which the incumbent is unwilling to continue to provide.

---

2  Postal Act of 22 December 1997, Articles 14-17.

## 4. **Price and quality**

The price and the quality of the universal service, as defined above, are subject to certain constraints imposed by the Directive. Other postal services are not in these respects regulated at the European level.

### Price

The Directive sets (in Article 12) a number of principles, with which Member States are required to ensure that the pricing of the universal service complies. These are that the price of the universal service should be:

- affordable;
- related to the cost of providing it;
- transparent; and
- non-discriminatory.

Member States are given the right, but not the obligation, to retain uniform pricing for postal services within their territory. It will be interesting to see whether any of them elect to move away from uniform pricing. It is a highly unusual requirement: even telecommunications in the public sector commonly has different price bands related to distance, or at least for local and non-local calls. The only Member State whose national Post Office has had formally different prices for local and national mail, Spain, abandoned the distinction in 1998. Many believe that effective liberalisation of the postal services market is incompatible with maintenance of a uniform price. Certainly the discounts now offered in some areas of competitive postal services, like direct mail in several Member States, already seem hard to reconcile with uniform pricing, under which discounts should reflect only saved costs, for example, as the result of pre-sorting by the user.

### Quality

The Directive lays down specific quality standards only in one respect, speed, and only for cross-border mail between Member States (Article 18 and Annex). 85% of items weighing up to 20kg posted from one Member State to another must be delivered by the third working day after posting, and 97% by the fifth day.

A study of cross-border mail was undertaken last year for the European Commission by PricewaterhouseCoopers: "Liberalisation of incoming and outgoing intra-Community cross-border mail", December 1998. This suggests, citing a study by the International Post Corporation, that the standards set in the Directive were not met in 1996 in any Member State in respect of cross-border mail from all others[3]. Of course each national Post Office can only affect the time an item of mail takes on its own territory, unless it undertakes the carriage of outgoing cross-border mail from other Member States which is destined for addresses in its home country, as several do for business customers. It is far from clear how the standards set in the Directive will be enforced, nor how it will be judged to what extent the fault lies with the sending or the receiving Member State.

Member States are required to establish, publish, monitor and enforce quality standards for other, domestic aspects of the universal service, including:

- speed, regularity and reliability (Article 16);
- the handling of customer complaints (Article 19); and
- nforming customers about prices and quality levels (Article 6).

## 5. Further liberalisation

The Directive calls on the European Parliament and the Council to decide by 1 January 2000 on "the further gradual and controlled liberalisation of the postal market" (Article 7). To initiate this process, the Commission has undertaken a review of the sector and will shortly make a formal proposal. Three particular areas of possible liberalisation are singled out in the Directive: cross-border mail, direct mail and reduction in the weight and price limits of the reserved area. The last is a step behind the others in the wording of the Directive.

To carry out the review, the European Commission has appointed consultants to undertake a series of studies over the last year. Two of these have already been mentioned, by NERA on the cost of the universal service and by PricewaterhouseCoopers on cross-border mail. The remaining studies in the series are:

- "On the liberalisation of clearance, sorting and transport" by CTcon (Germany), published in August 1998;

---

3 PricewaterhouseCoopers, "Liberalisation of incoming and outgoing intra-Community cross-border mail" (December 1998), Table 2.9, p 29.

- "Direct Mail" by Arthur Andersen (Spain), published in October 1998;
- "Study on the weight and price limits of the reserved area in the postal sector" by CTcon (Germany), published in November 1998; and
- "Modelling the impact of liberalisation of postal services" by MMD (UK), published in February 1999.

In proposing the likely direction of future liberalisation the European Commission will no doubt seek to synthesise the findings of each of these studies into a coherent overall policy.

**Network access**

The CTcon study on the liberalisation of clearance, sorting and transport deals with an aspect of market liberalisation which has been very important in other utility services: the question of access for other operators to the network of the existing monopoly provider. It has been almost a defining characteristic of utilities that they are provided through a network which has at least elements of natural monopoly. It is not, for example, economic for anyone else to build and maintain a network of electricity transmission lines or gas pipelines. In such a case, the network which has a natural monopoly may remain under the sole control of the incumbent monopoly provider, which decides whether to let anyone else use it, and, if so, on what terms. But if that is the case, then competitive entry even to the parts of the market which do not have natural monopoly may be effectively deterred. The deterrent may be either the fear or the reality that the terms on which competitors get to use the core network will never be as good as the terms on which the network owner's own services use it.

The CTcon study of this question in the postal sector finds economies of scale – and thus elements of natural monopoly – primarily in the delivery of mail. Collection also has some, though they are less marked, and perhaps only hold over a relatively short period. Sorting and transport do not exhibit economies of scale, though there may be a little lumpiness, for a time, in investment in sorting machinery.

Even in delivery, of course, very little of the network is fixed in the sense of a gas pipeline. In postal services, it is a matter of the number of people, transport vehicles and delivery offices which constitute the delivery network, and all of those could fairly readily find something else to do. What fixes a postal network is the desired or regulated frequency of collection and delivery, and the number of collection and delivery points. The frequency, and the number of points, are subject to change, either for commercial or for non-commercial reasons. There is a cost to being able to deliver letters every day to every address, whether or not any letters are in practice delivered. It cannot be economic to be able to do so unless in practice a lot of letters are delivered to a lot of addresses on most days.

The study looks at a number of the practical difficulties which would be involved in any attempt to oblige the incumbent to accept mail into its network at the delivery stage, or any earlier stage of the value chain. It concludes that these difficulties can be overcome, though with some difficulty, and not necessarily at every stage of the value chain. The study does not distinguish between outward and inward sorting, and it makes but does not pursue the point that it might not be operationally feasible to have competitor access just at the distribution stage (after inward sorting). It treats the question of access in practice as purely a question of access to the delivery stage. This represents an average of 55% of the costs of EU Post Offices, the range between them going from 43% to 69%.

In terms of the likely consequences of obliging Post Offices to offer network access on regulated terms to their competitors, the study's main findings are as follows:

(1) The effect is likely to be limited to bulk ordinary (non-direct) letter mail from businesses. Direct mail is unlikely to be affected, on the grounds that direct mail originators already undertake much of the work upstream of delivery. This is an important point. It is not an obvious one. It may be influenced by the elision in the study between outward and inward sorting. Direct mailers certainly often undertake much of the outward sorting of their mail, but inter-regional transport and inward sorting are less commonly done by anyone other than the national Post Office.

(2) The effect is likely to be negligible. Where it is more than that, the most likely outcome is a loss of market share not exceeding 10% and a fall in price on bulk business mail not exceeding 5%[4] (the study does not think universal pricing can survive network access liberalisation[5]). On a further set of assumptions about the profitability of the business in question, CTcon estimates that that

---

4 CTcon, "On the liberalisation of clearance, sorting and transport" (August 1998) 61-65.
5 *Ibid*, 27-28.

would reduce Post Office profits by some 3.6% on average, the range being from 1.9% to 5.8%. Given present average profitability of 3%, such a fall is not insignificant, but as CTcon concludes, it "does not endanger the stability of the postal system".[6]

3. Network access is unattractive to national Post Offices and only of limited attractiveness either to potential competitors or to postal regulators. CTcon accordingly recommends against this as the way forward for liberalisation of the European postal market.

## Direct mail

Direct mail currently represents around a quarter of total mail in the "reservable" area in the European Union. It is much the fastest growing segment of the postal services market. It is already liberalised – that is, fully open to operators other than the national Post Office to carry – in a third of the Member States.

The direct mail study by Arthur Andersen starts by reviewing the nature of direct mail communication and the various players who take part in the direct mail market. It summarises the current situation in the direct mail market and assesses the main strengths and weaknesses in the different Member States. It relates future growth in direct mail to a number of different indicators. Some of these are external:

- economic indicators, principally the growth in gross domestic product;
- demographic indicators, principally the growth in numbers of households;
- social indicators, primarily the involvement of women in the labour force;
- technology factors, including the development of the databases which are used in direct mail and the relative attractiveness of direct mail against other forms of communication.

Other indicators are internal to the direct mail market, principally:

- the attitudes and expectations of the various players in the market;
- the degree of development of the postal infrastructure in the Member State concerned;

---

6 *Ibid*, 10.

  ▪ public acceptance of direct mail by recipients in the Member
    State concerned.

In drawing conclusions about the likely future of the direct mail
market, the study divides Member States into three categories, highly
attractive ("A"), attractive ("B"), and moderately attractive ("C").
Further loss of market share by the national Post Office in the Member
States which have already liberalised direct mail is not expected to be
significant. In newly liberalised markets, the loss of market share by the
national Post Office is expected to vary by category. In category C
Member States the national Post Office is expected to have a 9%
smaller share of both volume and revenue by 2007 if direct mail is
liberalised in 2003 than if the regulatory position remains unchanged.
In category A Member States the loss of market share is expected to be
11% of volume and 12% of revenue. Category B Member States lose
the most market share: 13% of volume and 16% of revenue.[7]

By 2007, full liberalisation of direct mail in 2003 is expected to have
increased total volumes of direct mail in category A Member States
across the European Union by 6%, while reducing total revenues by
8%, compared to the base case. In category B Member States, the study
predicts a 3-4% increase in volume and a 3-4% decrease in revenue.
For category C, volume rises by 4-5% while revenue falls by 3-4%.

Across the European Union as a whole, the study predicts that
liberalisation in 2003 would result in direct mail volumes almost 5%
higher by 2007 than under the status quo, with revenues from direct
mail 4.5% lower.[8] The study also predicts that the direct mail market will
grow fast enough for national Post Offices, in general, to be carrying
more direct mail and earning higher revenues from it in 2007 than in
1997, even under full liberalisation, despite their loss of market share.
This is not, however, expected to be the case in all Member States:
France, Germany and the United Kingdom are cited as exceptions.[9]

**Cross-border mail**

Cross-border mail within the European Union, which is the subject of
the PricewaterhouseCoopers study, represents on average only some
3% of total EU mail flows.

---

7 Arthur Andersen, "Study on the impact of liberalisation in the postal sector lot 1: direct mail"
   (November 1998), V-23.
8 *Ibid*, V-20.
9 *Ibid*, V-24.

Outward cross-border mail, from the originator to the border, is reported to be already liberalised, at least *de facto*, in most Member States. Completing the liberalisation of outward cross-border mail, and making it a legal requirement, are not expected to have much impact. The study estimates that shifting from *de facto* to *de jure* liberalisation here might cost national Post Offices 3% of their existing outward cross-border business. Where there is no present liberalisation, it might cost them 10%.[10] Since these are generally proportions of small numbers, and outward cross-border mail is expected to grow by around 5% in the five years from 2001, formal liberalisation here will not much trouble most national Post Offices, nor much benefit most citizens. Luxembourg, where more than one-third of all mail is cross-border, may be a different matter, but it is not specially treated in the study.

Inward cross-border mail, from the border to the recipient, is more generally at present the preserve of the national Post Office. Only Finland and Sweden have so far liberalised it formally, and two more informally, Belgium and Ireland (which also has unusually important cross-border flows).[11] In the case of inward cross-border mail, the study predicts that liberalisation will reduce the market share of national Post Offices in their own markets from 100% to between 82% and 86% for the "inward" functions of inward sorting and delivery. Liberalisation of inward cross-border mail is also expected to cost national Post Offices an extra 10% of outward cross-border mail from their countries.[12] Again, these are not very large percentage reductions, and they are of small figures. In addition, national Post Offices are expected to be significant competitors in liberalised cross-border mail, so that what one loses another may gain.

The study concludes that "the liberalisation of cross-border mail in itself is not the main problem".[13] That is, the impact on existing cross-border mail will not be as important as two other impacts.

(1) A significant proportion of what is now domestic mail may become cross-border mail if cross-border mail is liberalised before domestic mail. Letters may be physically posted in one country to another to be posted back to the first (what is known in the trade as A-B-A remail) or, perhaps more likely, electronic messages may be sent from one country to another to generate physical messages which are posted

---

10 PricewaterhouseCoopers, *op cit*, Table 4.2, p 73.
11 *Ibid*, Table 2.3, p 18.
12 *Ibid*, Table 4.2, p 73.
13 *Ibid*, 72

back. The study judges that up to 30% of domestic mail is potentially convertible in this way, and that up to 70% of that may in fact be converted. 30% of domestic mail is, on average, ten times the volume of existing cross-border mail within the European Union. The impact on national Post Offices is reduced as the study also assumes that up to 80% of this induced cross-border mail would be given back to the national Post Office in the receiving country to deliver.[14]

(2) Once inward cross-border mail is liberalised there will be a strong temptation for new entrants into that market to carry domestic mail as well.[15] That would improve the economies of scale of their delivery operations, even if domestic mail had not yet been formally liberalised. This boundary is likely to be very hard for regulatory authorities to police: how do you prove that a particular envelope has not come across a border?

### Lowering the weight threshold

A second study by the German consultants CTcon has looked at the liberalisation of the domestic mail market by way of lowering, or even removing, the price or weight thresholds below which mail is reserved to the national Post Office. This kind of liberalisation goes directly to the essential aspect of the monopoly currently exercised by most national Post Offices. Yet it also, in practice, has a number of "easy wins". The limit set by the existing Directive is 350g. It is possible to reduce that limit significantly without affecting large volumes of mail.

Weight limits are described in the study as the better alternative to price limits, largely on the grounds that they are easier to police. Stamp prices may be visible, but discounts given to customers, for example, at the end of a period, are not. The study points out that introducing a general limit of 100g for all items of correspondence would keep 94% of the volume and about 85% of the revenue in the reservable area. A 50g limit would keep 85% of the volume and 77% of the revenue in the reservable area.[16]

The study also looks in some detail at which sorts of mail flows would be likely to attract competitors if they were allowed in. For this purpose mail flows in each Member State are divided by user type

---

14 *Ibid*, Table 4.3, p 80.
15 *Ibid*, 62.
16 CTcon, "Study on the weight and price limits of the reserved area in the postal sector" (November 1998), 32-34.

(business or household) and by location of sender and recipient (urban or rural). The study asserts that the flows of interest to competitors are likely to be urban-urban flows, urban to rural flows from business senders, and rural to urban flows of non-direct mail from business senders. Across the European Union as a whole, these "attractive"" flows represent three-quarters of all mail below 350g.[17] The implication here is that liberalisation by lowering weight-band thresholds will leave the national Post Office carrying:

- all mail below the new reserved threshold;
- the "unattractive" quarter of mail in the newly liberalised weight-bands; and
- that share of the contested, "attractive" mail in the newly liberalised weight-bands which competitors do not succeed in taking.

This further limits the effect of liberalising all but the lowest weight-bands, which contain most mail. A 20g limit, for example, is calculated to leave only 22% of the volume and 29% of the revenue from all mail below 350g in categories which are both liberalised and attractive.[18] If competitors took 10% of this contested part of the market, they would thus be taking 2-3% of the volume and revenue of the national Post Office.

In looking at how much of newly-contestable mail flows competitors might in practice take, CTcon have suggested four scenarios. Broadly, these range from high-quality existing operators who cut their prices in a successful attempt to preserve volume market share, to low-quality existing operators who lose significant market share but keep their prices largely unchanged because the competition is on quality grounds. The four scenarios are:

(1) price reductions of up to 25% with volume loss of up to 5%;

(2) price reductions of up to 15% with volume loss of up to 10%;

(3) price reductions of up to 10% with volume loss of up to 25%;

(4) price reductions of up to 5% with volume loss of up to 50%.

All four scenarios are applied to each Member State, though clearly not all are equally likely in each case, and the last is an improbable, extreme case without support in the evidence gathered from those countries

17 *Ibid*, 36.
18 *Ibid*, Figures 7-8, p 38.

which have already liberalised their mail. This scenario is described as relevant only where competitors are able to come in competing hard both on quality and on price.

The study takes the estimated loss of market share on into its effect on the profitability of national Post Offices. To do that, CTcon have had to make a number of important assumptions, such as that:

- profitability of reserved mail business is the same as reported profitability for the whole business of the national Post Office, which in some Member States includes telecommunications and in all of them includes significant non-mail business;
- transport costs and manual sorting costs vary directly with volume but automated sorting costs only vary half as much as volume;
- 80% of delivery costs are fixed while 20% vary directly, up and down, with changes in volume.

On the basis of the assumptions made, the study calculates the impact on profitability of each of the four scenarios. The growth in the mail market over the next 10 years assumed in this study offsets the loss of profit from liberalisation in almost all cases. If three-quarters of total costs are fixed, then any volume growth is very profitable. A weight limit reduced to 20g, on the assumptions used, leaves aggregate profitability across the European Union higher in 2007 than in 1997. Only a weight-limit of 0g, that is the full liberalisation of all mail flows, is shown as producing aggregate losses by 2007, of 4% under the second scenario and 8-9% under the first and third.[19]

## Next steps

MMD's part has been to prepare a computer-based model to help the European Commission in coming to a view on the next stage of liberalisation to propose. The model has drawn on all of the individual studies discussed above. It has been designed to replicate the findings of each study on the basis of the assumptions used in that study, but also to allow a common set of assumptions to be used, for instance about market growth. The model allows any number of liberalisation scenarios to be run, with different combinations of type and timing of liberalisation, and different assumptions about the price and quality offer of competitors and the response of national Post Offices.

---

19 *Ibid*, Table 9, p 44.

The primary output of the model is the volume of mail of different kinds carried by different types of operator, and the revenue they earn from it. It also takes this on into the implications for both employment and profitability, but only on the basis of a whole series of further assumptions. MMD have sought to make the assumptions used explicit and simple. They are designed as first approximations of the differences in these respects between the different liberalisation scenarios which the European Commission, and later others, may wish to consider.

The model starts from predictions for the postal services market across the European Union if there is no further liberalisation after the February 1999 deadline for implementation of Directive 97/67/EC. These show significant growth in the volume of mail carried by national Post Offices. Ordinary letter mail traffic, for all the European Union Post Offices taken together, although not for all of them individually, is expected to grow by 15% over the next 10 years. Direct mail is expected to grow by more than 50%. Total market growth is expected to be slightly faster than for the national Post Offices. Employment in postal services, on the assumptions used in the model, is expected to grow slightly both in national Post Offices and in private-sector providers. Some Post Offices make money, some lose it. In aggregate, the status quo is expected to see Post Office profits more than double over the 10 years.

At the other end of the spectrum, the model predictions for the impact of full liberalisation from 1 January 2003 of all postal services are that:

- revenue for national Post Offices from ordinary letter mail still, in aggregate, rises, though more slowly than volume as prices are cut to maintain market share, and significantly less than revenue from direct mail;
- total market revenues fall slightly, compared to the status quo, as lower prices outweigh higher volumes;
- mployment in national Post Offices falls, though not dramatically, and overall employment in postal services still rises a little as competitors take on more staff;
- the profit margin on what is at present reserved postal business for national Post Offices shrinks, in aggregate, to no more than 1%, with seven out of the 15 individually making losses (compared to three under the status quo).

Among the intermediate scenarios, those which involve cross-border mail (in any weight-band) being liberalised before domestic mail show very large increases in cross-border mail, as the result of the artificial shift across borders of what is now domestic mail, described above under "Cross-border mail".

The ball is now in the European Commission's court. At the time of writing, their new proposals are still expected shortly. Then the debate will be renewed again.

Peter Scott

# Economic Issues
# · in the Calculation of ·
# Dumping Duties

## Cliff Stevenson

The author is Chief Economist at Rowe & Maw, 20 Black Friars Lane, London EC4V 6HD. Telephone (44-171) 248 4282; cstevenson@roweandmaw.co.uk. The author wishes to thank Jeremy Kempton for his valuable comments on this article.

*European Economics & Law*
Palladian Law Publishing Ltd

# Economic Issues
# · in the Calculation of ·
# Dumping Duties

## 1. Introduction

On average, more than two–thirds of anti-dumping investigations initiated by the European Community result in the application of anti-dumping measures.[1] Whether the measures are in the form of anti-dumping duties or price undertakings, they must be based on the margin of dumping found for the investigation period, or a lower level if that would be sufficient to remove the injury. In order to impose anti-dumping measures, therefore, it is necessary to calculate both a dumping and an injury margin.

There is a good deal of literature produced on the economics of anti-dumping. However, most of it has focused on the conceptual questions of whether anti-dumping is an economically justified policy. Almost all of this work has been extremely critical of anti-dumping as a policy tool.

As a general rule, an economist that suggests that anti-dumping should be abandoned as a policy is not going to convince an anti-dumping authority to introduce better economics into its conduct of trade policy. Whatever one's opinion of the broader questions with regard to anti-dumping, the objective of introducing better economic input into the existing practices and procedures is surely desirable.

A small number of economists have started to look at the economics of anti-dumping law in a different way. Rather than automatically attacking the concept itself, this kind of work has focused on introducing more economic logic into existing law[2]. That said, very little time has been spent by economists looking at the calculation of dumping and injury margins.

---

1 During the period 1980-97, 67% of anti-dumping investigations initiated resulted in anti-dumping measures.

2 Examples include Tom Hoehn and Céline Peltier "Demonstrating causation in trade disputes", J Miranda "Should anti-dumping laws be dumped?" (1996) *Law and Policy in International Business* Vol 28, Fall issue. Peter Holmes with Jeremy Kempton "Study on the economic and industrial aspects of anti-dumping policy", Sussex European Institute Working Papers in Contemporary European Studies (No 22).

Many people consider that the dumping calculation is defined in such a detailed way in Article 2 of the EC anti-dumping Regulation[3] that there is little scope for economists to get involved. The purpose of this article is to show that this view is in fact incorrect. Despite the fact that Article 2 (which is closely based on Article 2 of the WTO Anti-Dumping Agreement) does set out a detailed method by which the dumping margin should be calculated, most of the provisions nevertheless contain some element of discretion. The legal interpretation of such "grey" areas, while important, is not sufficient to ensure a logical approach to the calculation.

The first objective of this article is, therefore, to set out certain elements of the dumping calculation where economic interpretation and analysis are necessary.

The second part of the article looks at the calculation of the injury margin. In this case, there is very little literature on the subject at all. While several people have analysed aspects of the dumping calculation, few have written about the injury margin calculation[4]. Therefore, from both a legal and economic viewpoint, the injury margin merits more attention than it currently receives. This article will concentrate on identifying some of the economic issues arising out of the injury margin calculation.

The article will argue that there are many issues in both the dumping and injury calculations where economic judgement is required.

It will, in effect, provide a practical checklist of issues where economic discretion is needed. The emphasis is on the practical element of this analysis. These are not necessarily issues where economic theory or concepts are by themselves prescriptive. In many cases, it is about the economist ensuring that there is economic logic to the decisions when discretion has been exercised. In reviewing such issues, it is assumed that the objective of the dumping and injury calculations is to produce the most accurate representation of the level of dumping and injury practised (as currently defined under EC and WTO law). No judgements are made on the economic rational of the law as it stands.

---

3 Council Reg 384/96 as amended by Regs 2331/96 and 905/98.
4 An exception is Edwin Vermulst and Paul Waer, "The calculation of injury margins in EC anti-dumping proceedings (1991) *Journal of World Trade*, December.

## 2. **Economic issues in the calculation of the dumping margin**

### Normal value

*Representativeness test*

In order for prices derived from domestic sales to be considered "representative for the market concerned" a guideline is set (Article 2(2)). Where the sales volume of domestic sales of the product concerned is more than 5% of the exports to the EC, the prices are considered to be representative.

A lower volume of sales can be used where, despite failing the "5% test", the prices can still be considered to be representative.

Although this is a clear guideline on determining whether domestic prices are representative, there are questions as to how the test should be applied in practice?

First, there is the situation where prices can still be considered representative despite the 5% threshold not being met. The general purpose of the 5% test is to ensure that domestic sales are not so small (relatively) as to render the prices unreliable. However, it is not clear by what criteria sales less than 5% can be considered to be made at representative prices. In practice, when domestic sales are less than 5% of exports to the EC, they are not used. In such a situation, however, it is important to consider if there is a meaningful domestic market. This will require an economic assessment of the market circumstances of domestic sales which are likely to differ on a case-by-case basis.

Secondly, there is a question over whether this should be a one-stage or a two-stage test. The EC practice is to use a two-stage test: firstly global and then type–by–type. The global test is to ensure that total domestic sales are at least 5% of total export sales to the EC of the product concerned. The type–by–type test is to ensure that, for each type, the 5% level is also passed. This is a very restrictive interpretation of the provision and results in many situations where domestic prices that might be reliable are, in fact, rejected. The US practice, in contrast, is to apply the 5% test only on a global basis.

From an economic point of view, is the type-by-type test necessary? This again will depend on the particular circumstances. If a company sells 200 grades/types of screws on the EC and domestic market, yet only half of these are sold in representative quantities on the domestic market, there is a good chance that the prices of the other half would be reliable. In many cases there will be consistency between prices of the 200 types sold on the domestic market. As an example, 10 tons of type A and 10 tons of type B may be sold on the domestic market. If 100 tons of A is exported to the EC market, the 5% test is passed and domestic prices would be used. If 300 tons of B is sold on the EC market, the prices at which B is sold would not be considered representative under the EC's normal practice. A and B may differ by only a few millimetres on one dimension and be bought in similar quantities by the same domestic customers. In such a case, the domestic customers would expect B's price to be consistent with that of A. Whether such a situation exists is one of the issues that should be considered in deciding whether a type that does not pass the 5% test may still have representative domestic prices, rather than automatically rejecting the sales.

It can also be said that the global approach (as used in the US) may not always be appropriate. There may be reasons why there is no consistency in prices and therefore rejecting the prices of certain types where they have been sold in very small quantities, perhaps in unusual circumstances, may make the calculation a more accurate reflection of the actual level of dumping practised.

The two-stage approach of the EC in every case is perhaps too restrictive in that it can lead to the rejection of sales which may still produce representative prices. To the greatest extent possible actual price data from the exporter concerned should be used. The best approach may be a global 5% test, with the burden of proof reversed on the type by type test (*i.e.* all prices will be accepted if the global 5% test is passed unless for a particular type they can be shown to be unrepresentative).

## Assessment of whether prices are below the cost of production

Article 2(4) of Regulation 384/96 allows the exclusion of domestic sales below cost of production under certain conditions. A number of important economic issues arise in determining the cost of production.

The cost of production is clearly defined as being fixed and variable costs plus selling, general and administrative costs (Article 2(4)). Although some economists would like the concept of dumping to be based more on a measure of variable costs, it is clear that there is no room for interpretation in the overall concept of cost to be used (*i.e.* full average cost). Nevertheless, there is considerable room for economic input in determining the level of full average cost.

(1) There are two provisions in the EC anti-dumping Regulation which explicitly provide for cost of production to be adjusted. Article 2(5) provides that costs can be adjusted for non-recurring items of cost which benefit future and/or current production. Also, "start-up" costs can be taken out where new production facilities are used. Such adjustments to costs involve considerable discretion and it must be ensured that decisions, both in accepting and rejecting cost adjustments, are based on sound economic logic.

(2) A second issue concerns cost allocation methods where more than one product is produced. Methods used for accounting purposes within the company (often the basis of the Commission's approach) may not be appropriate in the context of anti-dumping investigations. Profitability at the level of individual grades or types (when there are many) could have no relevance to the company whatsoever. It is often the case that merely applying a company's allocation methods to calculate highly disaggregated cost and production data produces strange results. Discretion may have to be exercised in finding the most sensible allocation methods.

In this situation it may be reasonable to consider the pricing methods of the company. If the company does not check the profitability of each type but overall is making a profit for the product concerned, should it effectively be condemned if certain types are sold at a loss?

(3) A third issue relates to the effect of other factors on costs. For example, if there is a recession (which may well be a major factor in triggering the anti-dumping complaint), costs will have increased due to the fact that production falls and fixed costs are spread over a smaller base. If there is a recession, should costs be adjusted so as to be representative of costs in more normal market conditions?

(4) There is a question as to whether the representativeness test should be conducted after the cost of production test? If prices less than cost of production are excluded, and normal value is based on remaining sales at prices greater than cost, should the 5% representativeness test apply again? Is it certain that these sales could be considered to be representative if they are below 5% of export sales to the EC?

(5) We can question the use only of profitable sales to calculate normal value while excluding sales made at prices below cost. Should there be a minimum volume of sales at a profit? The issue discussed above

relates to this to some extent by asking if the 5% test should be applied after the cost of production test. However, the EC in practice applies a test which requires a minimum 10% of total domestic sales at a profit for them to be used. That is, if sales below cost are more than 90% of domestic sales, then the profitable transactions cannot be used. This differs in the United States where any profitable transactions can be used. Again, it is sensible to exercise discretion in assessing whether the profitable sales provide reasonable market prices, though it is not clear that a fixed percentage guideline is appropriate in all circumstances.

### Decision on alternative bases for normal value when domestic prices cannot be used

If prices cannot be used, what are the economic issues in choosing a proxy for domestic price (*i.e.* normal value)? The WTO Anti-Dumping Agreement (Article 2.2) provides for normal value either to be "constructed" from cost of production or to be based on export prices to a third export market. These two alternatives are incorporated in the EC anti-dumping Regulation (Article 2(3)).

There is no guidance as to which of these alternatives is preferable. From an economic point of view, is one more preferable than the other? If dumping is supposed to be related to the concept of a "fair price", cost of production would seem to be a better measure than export prices to other countries. For the latter, there is no guarantee that export prices to another country would be a good proxy for a non-dumped price. If the typical profit rate for the domestic market can be ascertained (from similar products or other producers), the cost of production plus profit is likely to be a much more accurate representation of the price that the products exported to the EC would be sold at if they were sold under normal conditions on the domestic market.

In using the constructed normal value approach, it is necessary to add a "reasonable amount" for profit. How should this profit rate be chosen? It is necessary to assess what the likely profit rate would be if the product was sold on the domestic market. This requires an assessment of the market conditions in order to estimate what the profit rate would be.

A further question arises as to whether there are other acceptable proxies for domestic price apart from the two explicitly mentioned in the WTO Anti-Dumping Agreement? The EC, for example, uses as a first choice the price of other producers in the domestic market (Article 2(1)). From an economic point of view this does not seem to be acceptable. Fair pricing can surely only be measured in terms of actual data from the firm concerned (assuming they are fully co-operating). Using prices of other companies might be acceptable as a last resort, but at least the two WTO methods mentioned above are derived from information produced by the actual company in question.

### Normal value for non-market economies

An extremely controversial issue arises in the case of assessing normal value for so-called "non-market economies". From an economic point of view, there is no problem with the rejection of prices from a non-market economy situation. The real problem arises in determining whether a country is a non-market economy or not. Regulation 905/98 sets out some criteria by which this decision can be taken (at least for China and Russia). The legal criteria that have been set out in the above-mentioned Regulation seem reasonable. The important economic question, therefore, is how, in practice, these criteria can be assessed. For example, how should it be assessed whether decisions of firms regarding prices, costs and inputs are made in response to market signals reflecting supply and demand?

### Treatment of related sales

It is the practice of the Commission to reject domestic sales made to related companies. Thus, if 75% of domestic sales are made through a related company, only the 25% independent sales will be used as the basis for calculating normal value. Important information is lost by excluding this information completely. This would seem to have no economic justification. All export prices are included in the dumping calculation (including related sales where export prices are "constructed" on the basis of selling prices from the first independent sale). There is no reason why it should not be the same for domestic prices. It may well be that a related sales company sells relatively large volumes to long-established customers, while the unrelated sales are smaller quantity transactions of a more ad hoc nature. In such a situation, by rejecting the related sales completely, the normal value perhaps becomes inflated upwards and not representative of the actual situation.

## Export price

There are fewer issues with regard to the export price than for the calculation of normal value. However, in cases where exports are made to related companies in the EC, the Commission will not use the transfer price and instead "constructs" export price from the first unrelated sale in the EC (Article 2(9)). However, the rejection of transfer prices does not necessarily have to be automatic. This is certainly not the case in other areas such as customs or tax issues. Therefore, the possibility should be genuinely open to show that transfer prices are not affected by the relationship. Constructing the export price from the first independent sale is not an exact science. It is necessary, for example, to subtract the profit and sales and general costs for the related company. Sometimes this is based on information from other companies, which opens the way for distortions to occur. If transfer prices can be shown to be reliable, they should be used, as they may represent the most accurate information available.

## Price comparison

A number of issues arise in making the comparison between export prices and normal value:

### *Should the comparison be done for the investigation period as a whole or for discrete periods within the investigation?*

An investigation period will be used for which all export and domestic prices will be collected (usually 12 months). The question is whether the calculation should made for the period as a whole? That is, should one average export price be compared to one average normal value (for each product type). In some cases this may well be appropriate. However, there may be economic circumstances which make this method unreliable. For example, if there is significant inflation throughout the investigation period, great care would have to be taken in making the price comparison. If the bulk of export sales are made at the end of the investigation period, while the largest proportion of domestic sales are made at the start of the investigation period (when inflation is lower), the level of dumping actually practised may be under-estimated if the calculation is done for the 12 months as whole (or vice versa). It may be more appropriate to make the comparison month by month.

If a month–by–month comparison is used, it is important that it is done on a reasonable basis. It may be, for example, that normal value is constructed on the basis of cost of production. If there is an average two-month gap between production and sales (i.e. where the product is held in stock), it would be better to use an appropriate lag in making the comparison.

Similar difficulties can arise when there are significant changes in exchange rates during the investigation period.

### In what circumstances should adjustments be made?

There is, of course, a strong legal obligation to make appropriate adjustments when it can be shown that price comparability and prices are affected.[5] It is often easier to establish that price comparability is affected than it is to know how the effect on prices should be assessed. In other words, how should necessary adjustments be valued?

This point raises an important question in relation to the WTO Anti-Dumping Agreement where it is stated that adjustments should be made when price comparability is affected (and not prices).[6] In the circumstances where it can be shown that price comparability is affected, but it is difficult to value, there can be no economic justification which would allow the rejection of the adjustment. Even if an adjustment is difficult to value, a best guess should be made to ensure that the calculation of dumping is as accurate as possible. This would seem to be the rationale behind the WTO formulation.

In this regard, certain adjustments are more straightforward than others. For example, credit, packing, and transportation costs can all relatively easily be identified and differences between domestic and export transactions measured. Other issues are more difficult in calculating a precise effect on prices. Examples are differences in quantities sold, differences in product specification and the differences in advertising activities between the domestic and export market. Each relevant adjustment requires an economic assessment of:

(1) whether there is a difference between the domestic and export sale that affects price comparability; and
(2) the best guess of the value of the adjustment required where it is not straightforward.

---

5 Article 2(10) of Reg 384/96.
6 Article 2.4 of WTO Anti-Dumping Agreement.

*Weighted average or transaction by transaction export price?*

The EC anti-dumping Regulation (Article 2(11)) requires that the comparison is normally established on the basis of a comparison of a weighted average normal value with a weighted average of all export prices. However, export prices can be compared to the weighted average normal value on a transaction by transaction basis if there is a pattern of export prices which differ significantly between different customers, regions or time periods.

The decision is an important one because, with a transaction by transaction export price, the Commission uses the controversial "zeroing" methodology (that is, positive dumping margins are counted as zero so that they do not offset the impact of targeted dumping). Thus, dumping margins will be higher when this method is used. There is discretion as to the criteria by which such differences are judged and it is important to assess if this approach is fully justified.

## 3. Economic issues in the calculation of the injury margin

### Why is an injury margin required?

Article 9(4) of the EC anti-dumping Regulation states that:

> "The amount of the anti-dumping duty shall not exceed the margin of dumping established but it should be less than the margin if such lesser duty would be adequate to remove the injury to the Community industry."

The implication of the lesser duty rule is that an "injury margin" must be calculated comparable to the dumping margin, allowing the lesser of the two to be used as the basis of the anti-dumping duty.

An injury margin is supposed to be representative of the level of injury caused by dumped imports. The problem is that injury can be shown in many different factors (see Article 3(5)) and it is not straightforward how all of the injury can be "captured" in one margin. However, the reality is that, in order to calculate an injury margin, a single non-injurious price for the dumped imports is required to compare against the dumped price.

The major difference between this and the dumping calculation, discussed above in Section 2, is the comparison of export price to the non-injurious price (NIP) in the injury margin calculation rather than normal value. The NIP is the price at which exports would no longer be causing injury. The extent to which the price of dumped imports undercuts the NIP is called the level of price underselling.

## Defining the non-injurious situation

We can use supply and demand analysis to help in identifying the non-injurious situation.

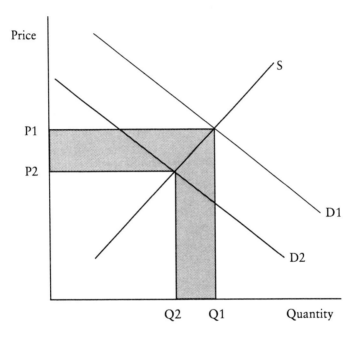

*Chart 1: EC industry supply and demand*

Demand and supply for the EC product are initially in equilibrium at P1Q1.

Where it is established that dumped imports are causing injury, this must mean that there is some substitution towards the dumped product from the domestic product. This means that at each given price, less of the EC product is demanded and therefore the demand curve shifts to the left (D2). In the above case this has resulted in a fall of both quantity sold and price. The extent to which the injury is predominantly shown in price or quantity sold depends on the elasticity of domestic supply and demand (*i.e.* slopes of the domestic supply and demand curves).

The key question, therefore, is what price increase is necessary for dumped imports in order to remove the injury caused by dumping? In the above example a measure of the injury caused is indicated by the shaded area. Assuming that there are no other causes of injury, the non-injurious price (NIP) is that which shifts the demand curve back to D1.

Of course, identifying the NIP is not necessarily straightforward. Whereas there are a number of ways in which normal value can be calculated, all of which are clearly set out in the EC anti-dumping Regulation, there is no such guidance on how the NIP should be calculated. The problem in providing such guidance is that it can be difficult to calculate a single price that will remove the injury, given that injury can be shown in a number of indicators.

This can be especially complicated when there are other causes of injury in addition to the dumping. In the situation as in chart 1, it may be that the demand curve has shifted further to the left due to injury caused by non-dumped imports as shown in chart 2. Also, reduced efficiency may have shifted the supply curve to the left. In this case "total" injury suffered by the EC industry will be Q1 to Q4, of which only Q1-Q2 is actually caused by dumped imports.

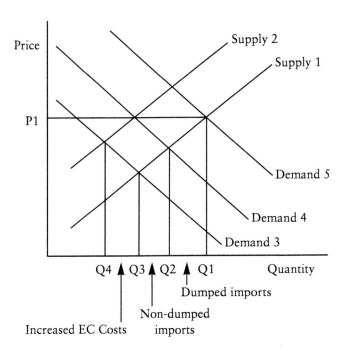

*Chart 2: Three causes of injury on the EC market*

In this case, unravelling the price that will remove the injury caused by dumping is more difficult. The objective of the NIP is clearly not to remove all injury. In such a case, however, how can it be certain that the NIP chosen is not removing more or less of the injury actually caused by dumping? This is a rather theoretical question and, from a practical point of view, it is unlikely that the injury margin calculation can be that precise.

## Principle method of calculation

### The standard method

One method has been used in the vast majority of cases and to this extent might be called the standard method.

Under the standard method, the NIP is established on the basis of the weighted average cost of production of the EC industry making a complaint, plus a reasonable profit margin.

Cost of production includes fixed and variable costs, as well as sales and general administrative expenses (SGA). The usual method is to take these costs for each producer supporting the complaint and calculate a weighted average.

Four issues are extremely important in determining the non-injurious price using the standard method.

### The determination of whose costs should be used in the calculation

There is a question over which costs should be used for the purpose of calculating the NIP. It may not be reasonable, for example, to include the most inefficient producers in calculating the average EC costs, as a price based on their costs may be totally unachievable in a competitive market.

A further issue with regard to cost of production is the extent to which there may be dynamic aspects in the process of removing injury. If an anti-dumping duty allows an EC industry to increase production, its cost per unit will fall. This should be taken into account in calculating the non-injurious price to ensure the EC producers are not "over-compensated" for the injury they have suffered.

### Comparison between dumped product and that produced by EC industry

A major problem that must be addressed in the injury threshold calculation is the comparison between the dumped product and that produced by EC industry. Comparison between the export and domestic models for the dumping calculation can be difficult enough, but at least in that case the comparison is usually with models produced by the same company.

For the purpose of the injury threshold calculation, the price comparison is between the dumped import and the equivalent EC product. Matching different types/models can be extremely difficult especially with heavily differentiated (*e.g.* branded) products.

A major issue in undertaking this calculation is, therefore, making appropriate adjustments to the export price and EC costs to ensure a fair comparison.

Particularly important are adjustments to ensure that the comparison is made at the same level of trade. However, the list of possible adjustments set out in Article 2(10) of the EC anti-dumping Regulation should all be considered to see if any of them are relevant. When products are differentiated an estimate of the value of differences must be made, which may involve an assessment of consumer perceptions.

## Profit margin used in calculation

Whether a particular profit rate is reasonable depends on the particular context. This involves an assessment of issues such as the maturity of the product in question and the need for future investment. There are no guidelines as to how this decision should be made (except to some extent, precedents set in previous cases). It is important therefore, that an accurate and detailed assessment of a normal profit rate for the industry and market in question is made. This is a variable which can have a particularly significant impact on the dumping calculation.

An interesting issue is the extent to which the profit rate used should be that which would apply in a competitive market, even where the "EC industry" concerned is a monopolist who could earn monopoly profits if import competition is effectively removed.

## Taking account of other causes of injury

In theory, the injury margin should only remove injury caused by dumped imports. Injury caused by other factors should not be incorporated within the injury margin. The question remains, however, as to how this should be done.

A particularly troublesome case arises in the situation where it is found that the dumping margin is less than the injury margin. In this situation, it is clear that if the dumping margin was zero, there would still be injury as measured by the price underselling measure. The NIP in this situation is, therefore, open to serious question as to the accuracy of what it is supposed to represent (*i.e.* removing the injurious effect of dumping).

## Is there an economic logic behind this method?

There are a number of requirements for this method to produce a calculation based on sound economic logic:

- the break even price with a reasonable profit is the one that removes injury caused by dumping;
- increased price of dumped imports to this level allows EC producers to increase their price to this level also;
- products are homogenous (perfect substitutes) or all necessary adjustments can be accounted for.

The removal of injury requires that the measures adopted allow the Community industry to realise sales on the basis of prices at a non-injurious level (*i.e.* to be able to increase prices to profitable levels without loss of sales volume). If the above conditions are met, the NIP based on weighted average cost of production of Community industry is a reasonable basis on which to calculate the injury margin.

It is reasonable because, if products are perfect substitutes, increasing the price of one of them would allow the price of the other to be increased. In commodities, for example, where world prices are set according to demand and supply in the market, it is not possible for EC and non-EC prices to differ. If dumping is taking place, in order to maintain sales, the EC industry must lower its price to the dumped price or it will make no sales whatsoever. Thus, increasing the price of dumped imports should allow the EC industry to increase its prices.

The method becomes more complicated if there are other causes of injury (as shown in Chart 2 above), as the objective should only be to remove injury caused by dumping.

In the case where products are differentiated then it is not evident that EC producers will be able to increase their prices to this level. If there are differences between the products, equalising the actual prices in this way does not necessarily make economic sense.

Of course, if adjustments are made for all the differences, the adjusted prices are equalised but the actual prices remain differentiated. However, how should non-price factors be handled? For example, consumers may perceive the EC product to be better than the imported product and therefore may be prepared to pay a premium for it. To this extent, it is not reasonable to equalise the prices as this will shift a disproportionate amount of sales to the EC industry. However, as with adjustments in the dumping calculation, there is a problem of how the value of such factors should be measured.

In such situation, to estimate the NIP accurately it will be necessary to have detailed information on demand and supply conditions (including elasticities) for the economic logic of the calculation to hold. Currently this level of data does not exist within a typical anti-dumping investigation, though there are methods by which reasonable estimates might be made.

### There can be no one method of calculating the injury margin

The main conclusion that emerges from the above is that there can be no one method of calculation the NIP and, therefore, the injury margin. Depending on the circumstances, determining the NIP may actually be a complex economic problem requiring much more data than currently is collected.

That this is true is proven by the fact that there are even situations where the Commission has recognised that the standard method is not appropriate to calculate the injury margin and an alternative method has been used.[7] However, such cases are relatively rare.

It is clear, therefore, that there should be more debate on meaningful alternatives to calculate the NIP, to ensure that the obligations of the lesser duty rule are properly implemented in every instance.

## 4. Conclusion

The article has shown that, in both the calculation of the dumping and injury margins there is considerable room for discretion and a consequent need for good economic input to ensure that logical decisions are made. This is an extremely important conclusion, as each occasion on which discretion must be exercised can have a significant impact on the final calculations.

---

7 See particularly compact disk players from Japan and Korea (Reg 112/90) and audio tapes from Japan Korea and Hong Kong (Reg 1251/91).

This clearly dispels the view that economists have nothing to contribute to the debate over the level of an anti-dumping duty (or a price undertaking). In fact, it can be stated that their input here is probably most valued in terms of all aspects of the investigation, as logical and consistent economic decisions with regard to these calculations will ensure that dumping margins are set at the fairest level possible.

Cliff Stevenson

# EU-CEEC Trade Relations:
·   From Anti-Dumping   ·
to Competition?

## Jeremy Kempton and Dr Peter Holmes

Jeremy Kempton is an economist at Rowe & Maw, 20 Black Friars Lane, London EC4V 6HD. Telephone (44-171) 248 4282; jkempton@roweandmaw.co.uk

Dr Peter Holmes is Jean Monnet Reader in the Economics of European Integration, Sussex European Institute, University of Sussex, Brighton BN1 9QN, United Kingdom. Telephone (44-1273) 606755; p.holmes@sussex.ac.uk.

*European Economics & Law*
Palladian Law Publishing Ltd

# EU-CEEC Trade Relations: · From Anti-Dumping · to Competition?

## 1. Introduction

### Why might competition policy remove the need for anti-dumping?

There is a long held belief among economists that the international application of competition policy (or the application of international competition policy) would provide a way to do away with the most widely used and probably most criticised instrument of contingent protection: the EU's anti-dumping instrument.[1]

In the discussions before the preparation of the Europe Agreements many outside economists and some in the Commission felt that the application of EU–style competition rules by the associated states was a necessary and sufficient condition for the ending of the use of anti-dumping by both sides. The logic behind this is that the type of predatory pricing which many think anti-dumping should deal with, should equally well be dealt with under competition rules.

Such an approach was, however, rejected in the final position adopted by the EU. The 1991 Europe Agreements between the Community and, now 10, Central and East European countries provide for the removal of many instruments of trade protection.[2] However, the option of introducing some sort of protection, in the form of anti-dumping measures, remains and has continued to be used since the agreements were reached. Although some attempts have been made to reduce the incidence of the instrument, the pressures for retaining such an option of protection are great,

---

1  See *e.g.* P Nicolaides, "Does the international trade system need anti-dumping rules?" (1990) *World Competition*, September issue; P Messerlin, "Should anti-dumping rules be replaced by national or international competition rules?' (1995) *World Competition*, Vol 18(3).
2  Bulgaria, Czech Republic, Estonia, Hungary, Latvia, Lithuania, Poland, Romania, Slovak Republic, Slovenia.

particularly from certain specific, but often influential, sectors, such as basic steel and chemicals.

In this article we explain the political and legal logic that underlies this. We will explain the differences between the basic philosophies of trade and competition policy and show why it is hard to expect the EU to abandon unconditionally the use of trade measures before countries accede to the EU without a major political breakthrough which goes beyond that which we have seen so far.

## Anti-dumping and regional integration

In two earlier examples of economic integration in Europe, the European Economic Area (EEA) and the European Union itself, the adoption of common competition rules has led to the removal of other instruments of trade policy. In the case of the EU, for example, competition and state aids rules within the common market along with the abolition of tariffs, non-tariff barriers and other forms of protection meant that commercial policy measures like anti-dumping became unnecessary. Similarly, the signing of the EEA covering the four freedoms of the single market removed tariffs and largely left competition rules to regulate any remaining private barriers to trade (although in the case of the EEA the fisheries sector was excluded – see below).

A further, non-European, example of this took place as a part of the Australia-New Zealand Closer Economic Relations Agreement (ANZCERTA) where, in 1990, it was agreed to stop the use of the anti-dumping instrument as an element of the existing wider free trade agreement.

As Miranda points out, many people see such a replacement following "pretty much automatically on the heels of the creation of a free trade agreement".[3]

The basic premise behind this is an obvious one, if in practice, often less clear. Where free trade exists between two countries the ability to resell back into the exporting (higher-priced) market at the dumped prices should mean that the dumping becomes ineffective. It is, indeed, a long-argued point by economists that effective application of competition rules would remove the need for instruments of protection

---

3  J Miranda, "Should anti-dumping laws be dumped?" (1996) *Law and Policy in International Business*, Vol 28(1) Fall issue.

at all, since anti-dumping should, it is held,[4] only be used to combat predatory pricing. In 1997 Canada and Chile adopted a bilateral Free Trade Agreement which, in fact, goes even further by eliminating the use of anti-dumping measures without there being any such replacement by competition rules. The argument here is that predatory international dumping is so rare, and would be so difficult in this case, that attempting to introduce an over-arching competition mechanism would not be worth the trouble.[5]

In so far as both policies are dealing with economic efficiency, the notion that competition rules could replace anti-dumping ones might be plausible. Indeed, the original principle behind anti-dumping, as outlined by Viner was an attempt to prevent predation, and thus making it in this sense more akin to competition rules.

However, it has become increasingly clear throughout the history of the two policies that today they are not dealing with the same issues. As such, the possibility of incorporating the model of the EU, the EEA or ANZCERTA and doing away with anti-dumping measures altogether may still be some way off.

## Nature of the two policies

The differences between the two policies which have emerged are usually characterised in the literature in terms of competition rules preserving competition and efficiency, whilst trade policy (including anti-dumping) offers protection to domestic firms against what is perceived as unfair competition from abroad.[6] In this sense one significant difference is the respective importance attached to producers, on the one hand, and consumers, on the other. This means that the two policies are in fact now addressing different economic situations and have different goals.

In particular, anti-dumping does not only respond to predatory pricing where monopolistic intent can be proved but rather to a number of examples of international price discrimination. It is in fact widely criticised for this, because price discrimination is a perfectly normal

---

4   Following Viner: J Viner, "Dumping: a problem in international trade" (1923). Reprinted Kelley, New York (1966).

5   For more on this see G Niels and A ten Kate, "Trusting anti–trust to dump anti–dumping: abolishing anti–dumping in Free Trade Agreements without replacing it with competition law" (1997) *Journal of World Trade*, Vol 31(6), December issue.

6   See *e.g.* B Hoekman and P Mavroidis, "Dumping, anti–dumping and anti–trust" (1996) *Journal of World Trade*, Vol 30(1), February issue.

aspect of business life and is not in any way illegal at the national or EU level. However, in the view of the European Commission, price discrimination between international markets provides evidence (a "rebuttable presumption") that the home market of the exporting firm is in some sense closed, providing the opportunity to cross-subsidise exports, or that there is some other form of asymmetric advantage.[7] Such an asymmetric advantage which is deemed to be unfair, could take many forms, from high tariffs to price or export controls on raw materials. Within the anti-dumping rules, the alleged victim is not under any obligation to specify what exactly this unfair advantage might be.

The crucial difference between price discrimination in the case of dumping and the variable prices within the EU is that the latter occur in the wider context of the EU rules on freedoms within the internal market, competition, state aids and so on, which imply, it is argued, that any price differences that occur cannot be the result of illegitimately acquired advantages.

For the Central and East European countries, the differences between competition rules and the anti-dumping instrument suggest, however, that the application of competition rules similar to those in place within the EU might not on its own be enough to warrant the complete removal of the anti-dumping instrument. Certainly the experience thus far *vis-à-vis* the CEECs has shown that, whilst there are moves to reduce the use of anti-dumping and to administer it in a slightly more favourable way, it has not been ruled out as a weapon of trade defence.

There are thus evolving stages in the trade relationship between the EU and the CEECs. First, in the past and up to the present trade policy, for example, in the form of anti-dumping, has been used extensively. A second stage corresponds with the current situation and the immediate future of trade relations in which we are seeing the early stages of a gradual phasing out and, in the meantime, a slightly more flexible application of the trade instruments as competition and other regulations are being adopted in the associated countries. Nonetheless, it would be misleading to suggest that competition rules are replacing trade policy whilst weapons like anti-dumping remain in place as possible courses of action. The third stage is then the future policy in the post-accession to the EU period. In this situation trade measures against one another will not be possible and the only recourse against perceived unfair trade will come through the application of the EU rules on competition.

---

7   See *e.g.* E Sakkers, "Anti-dumping and other trade instruments of the European Union: the involvement of industry", Address to the Euromin 1997 Conference, Barcelona, June 1997.

## 2. **Past and present use of the instrument**

The retention of the anti-dumping instrument in the Europe Agreements has been criticised for responding to protectionist demands from narrow sectoral interests. The nature of many of the industries involved (*e.g.* basic chemicals, steel etc) has meant that the Central and East European countries have tended to be some of the major targets of EU anti-dumping actions over the years.

The table in fact shows that the Central and Eastern European countries have been the major target of anti-dumping actions by the EU with roughly a third of cases opened in the last 15 years being against all Central and East European countries, and half of these being against the associated countries.

These figures indicate the importance of anti-dumping as a defence against imports from the CEECs, and also show that they have not necessarily declined as one might have expected. In the case of Poland, for example, five cases were opened between 1992 and 1995 which was as many as in the previous seven years, and a further three were opened from 1996-1998. Furthermore, from late 1997 to early 1999 various associated countries (most notably Poland) have been hit by definitive or provisional duties on six products (flat pallets of wood[8], steel tubes and pipes[9], unwrought zinc[10], hardboard[11], binder and baler twine[12], and steel ropes and cables.[13]

This said, the actual number of measures in force against the CEECs declined from 20 to 14 between the end of 1993 and the end of 1997 and the proportion of trade is affected by these measures is, in absolute terms, small. At the end of 1996, for example, the measures in force against the CEECs were reported by Stefano Micossi as concerning just 0.28% of total imports from these countries.[14] Of course, such a figure does not, however, give any indication of how much trade is deterred by the anti-dumping measures in place.

---

8  Flat Pallets of Wood from Poland. Definitive Duties: OJ 1997 L324.
9  Seamless Pipes and Tubes from the Czech Republic, Hungary, Poland, Romania, Russia and the Slovak Republic. Definitive Duties: OJ 1997 L322.
10 Unwrought, Unalloyed Zinc from Poland and Russia. Definitive Duties: OJ 1997 L272.
11 Hardboard from Bulgaria, Estonia, Latvia, Lithuania and Poland. Notice of Initiation: Definitive Measures: OJ 1999 L22.
12 Binder and Baler Twine from Poland, Czech Republic and Hungary: Provisional Measures: OJ 1998 L267.
13 Steel Ropes and Cables from Hungary and Poland: Provisional Measures: OJ 1999 L45.
14 See S Micossi Seminar on Trade Defence Instruments, Brussels, 27 January 1997.

| Anti-dumping investigations opened 1982-1998 | | | | | | | |
|---|---|---|---|---|---|---|---|
| | Total | Assoc Countries | Other C & E Europe | China | Japan | Other Asia | ROW |
| 1982 | 58 | 10 | 11 | 4 | 3 | 0 | 30 |
| 1983 | 38 | 8 | 8 | 2 | 4 | 2 | 14 |
| 1984 | 49 | 16 | 11 | 2 | 4 | 1 | 15 |
| 1985 | 36 | 6 | 8 | 1 | 2 | 4 | 15 |
| 1986 | 24 | 3 | 8 | 2 | 1 | 2 | 8 |
| 1987 | 39 | 3 | 5 | 0 | 7 | 10 | 14 |
| 1988 | 40 | 6 | 5 | 7 | 4 | 13 | 5 |
| 1989 | 27 | 6 | 3 | 5 | 2 | 6 | 5 |
| 1990 | 43 | 0 | 5 | 4 | 3 | 9 | 22 |
| 1991 | 20 | 4 | 2 | 4 | 5 | 3 | ·2 |
| 1992 | 39 | 3 | 10 | 8 | 0 | 11 | 7 |
| 1993 | 21 | 2 | 3 | 4 | 1 | 7 | 4 |
| 1994 | 43 | 6 | 7 | 5 | 2 | 12 | 11 |
| 1995 | 33 | 4 | 4 | 5 | 0 | 17 | 3 |
| 1996 | 25 | 3 | 1 | 6 | 0 | 5 | 10 |
| 1997 | 45 | 5 | 3 | 5 | 2 | 15 | 15 |
| 1998 | 20 | 6 | 3 | 1 | 0 | 4 | 7 |
| total 82-98 | 601 | 91 | 97 | 65 | 40 | 121 | 187 |

Source: Commission of the European Communities Annual Report on Anti-Dumping Activities, various years; Own data

* NB Associated countries = Bulgaria, Czechoslovakia (Czech Republic and Slovak Republic from 1993), Hungary, Poland, Romania, Lithuania (from 1992), Estonia (from 1992), Latvia (from 1992), Slovenia

Other Central and Eastern European countries = USSR (successor states from 1992), Yugoslavia (successor states from 1991), GDR (pre-1990)

"Other Asia" = Hong Kong, Indonesia, South Korea, Malaysia, Philippines, Singapore, Taiwan, Thailand, Vietnam

## Europe Agreements

The signing of the first Europe Agreements in 1991 laid down provisions for free trade in industrial goods between the EU and the CEECs. They also call for the adoption of EU-style competition rules in cases of behaviour affecting trade between the EU and the partner countries.

Notwithstanding these rules on competition, the Europe Agreements make no provision for doing away with the anti-dumping instrument. Indeed, they merely state that where dumping is taking place, action may be taken in accordance with Article VI of the GATT which deals with anti-dumping.[15]

The Commission Communication from July 1994 on the Europe Agreements and Beyond says in this regard that:

> "Once satisfactory implementation of competition and state aids policy has been achieved, *together with the application of other parts of Community law linked to the wider market,* the Union *could* decide to progressively *reduce* the application of commercial defence instruments for industrial products for the countries concerned" (emphases added).[16]

This clearly suggests that competition rules are not enough on their own, but rather that these wider (unspecified) aspects of Community law are crucial and that, even there, the elimination of measures cannot be guaranteed. This statement was repeated in the conclusions of the Essen Council of December 1994 with a slightly different wording, though apparently the same meaning ("the Union should be ready to consider refraining from using commercial defence instruments").[17] Paragraph 6.5 of the 1995 White Paper then reproduces exactly the statement from the July 1994 Commission Communication.[18] The mere fact that the obligation to make competition law compatible is one of the most explicitly highlighted features of the Europe Agreements should only serve to remind us that this is necessary but not to mislead us into thinking that it is sufficient.

Whilst in no way entirely removing the threat of anti-dumping, the EU has been attempting to act in a more flexible and favourable way towards these countries in its administering of the policy. This was most

---

15 See *e.g.* Europe Agreement with Poland, Article 29, OJ 1993 L348.

16 COM (94) 320 final, 13 July 1994.

17 Council of the European Union (1994), Essen European Council, Conclusions of the Presidency, Annex IV.

18 White Paper on the Preparation of the Associated Countries of Central and Eastern Europe for Integration into the Internal Market of the Union, COM (95) 163 final, 3 May 1995 and COM (95) 163 final/2, 10 May 1995.

explicitly outlined in the Essen Council conclusions of December 1994 in which a willingness to accept price undertakings rather than imposing duties was expressed. The Essen conclusions called, in addition, for an "early warning system" whereby more information is to be passed on and discussion to take place at an earlier stage in cases involving Associated Countries. This allows the governments in the relevant countries to inform their producers that a complaint has been made and provide them with the opportunity to start preparing for it, although how much of an advantage this has actually proved to be in practice is open to question.

The Europe Agreements with, initially, Hungary, Poland and the former Czechoslovakia and now the other associates all called for the adoption within three years of their entry into force of legislation in each partner country to mirror the competition provisions (anti-trust and state aids) of the Treaty of Rome. But let us be clear what is being asked for. The Polish Europe agreement is typical in stating (our italics) that:

> "**63.1** The following are incompatible with the proper functioning of the Agreement, *in so far as they may affect trade between the Community and [CEEC country]*:
>
> i.  all agreements between undertakings, decisions by associations of undertakings and concerted practices between undertakings which have as their object or effect the prevention, restriction or distortion of competition;
> ii. abuse by one or more undertakings of a dominant position in the territories of the Community or of [CEEC country] as a whole or in part thereof;
> iii. any public aid which distorts or threatens to distort competition by favouring certain undertakings or the production of certain goods... .
>
> **63.2** Any practice contrary to this Article shall be assessed on the basis of criteria arising from the rules and Articles 85, 86 and 92 of the Treaty establishing the European Community."

The legal obligation is thus not to harmonise competition laws but to adopt competition rules that will not have the effect of "distorting" trade between the EU and the CEEC partners. The obligation is to prevent absence of competition rules or their lack of enforcement from allowing private or public barriers to market entry arising. Competition law is highlighted because of its potential cross border impact, not because it can replace trade policy.

The Director General of DG III of the Commission has shed more light on the contrast between competition rules and wider aspects of the *acquis communautaire* with respect to anti-dumping rules in calling for commercial instruments to continue to play a role "up to the point where markets are substantially integrated".[19] He goes on to point out that this marks the difference between the CEECs and other trading partners as:

> "Since the establishment of the first Europe Agreements in the early nineties the declared aim has been economic and regulatory integration, and this aim has rapidly been supplemented by that of preparation for accession."

It is clear from these comments and above all from the statement in the July 1994 Commission Communication which was so widely reiterated that it is the overall "economic and regulatory integration" which will hold the key to the complete elimination of the anti-dumping instrument rather than the adoption of competition rules on their own.

## Undertakings

The EU anti-dumping Regulation allows the Commission to accept price undertakings from firms as an alternative to the imposition of duties. Price undertakings mean that the dumping firms can offer to increase their prices by an amount sufficient to remove the injury being caused by the dumping. This provides the obvious advantage to the dumping companies that they receive the benefit from the ensuing price rise rather than it being paid by the purchaser as a tax.

Undertakings may be offered instead of provisional or definitive duties or, as is essentially the case in practice, can be suggested by the Commission. If they are accepted by the Commission (*i.e.* where the Commission is satisfied they will eliminate the injurious effect of the dumping and their acceptance is practical in terms of monitoring and implementation), the Anti-Dumping Advisory Committee is consulted.[20] Assuming no objection is raised, the anti-dumping investigation is terminated. Otherwise the Commission should make a proposal to the

---

19 See S Micossi Seminar on Trade Defence Instruments, Brussels, 27 January 1997
20 This Committee is a consultative body which is part of the Commission decision-making procedure. It is consulted at various stages of an anti-dumping investigation, principally at the opening, imposition of provisional measures and proposal for definitive measures stages (and also for the opening of reviews etc). It usually meets monthly in Brussels and is comprised of relevant civil servants from the national ministries of the 15 Member States.

Council of Ministers that the investigation be terminated which the Council must overturn by qualified majority. Where an existing undertaking is breached or withdrawn by the dumping party, a definitive duty can then be imposed (or a provisional duty in cases where the investigation into dumping and injury has not been concluded).[21]

The 1994 Essen Conclusions made a significant move with respect to undertakings by stating that the Commission "will give, on a case-by-case basis, where appropriate, a clear preference to price undertakings rather than duties".[22] This has since been extended by subsequent moves to give companies offering undertakings to manage those undertakings themselves.[23] It is highly unusual for the Commission to express such an *ex ante* preference for accepting undertakings (and indeed might even raise questions about the non-political nature of the instrument). Such a move is particularly significant given that the countries in question have until recently been deemed non-market economies in an anti-dumping proceeding. In the past, undertakings have not tended to be accepted from non-market economies largely due to the difficulties in ensuring they are respected.[24]

Even here, however, it should be noted that this concession on undertakings does not always work as a huge advantage to companies in the accession countries. Undertakings are not in practice the outcome of a negotiation between the two parties, but rather an imposed price by the Commission which the exporters can choose to accept or face duties. In a number of instances, companies find that the undertaking price which is set by the Commission is sufficiently high to prevent them from competing on the Community market.

## The EEA case

This reluctance on the part of the Community to go beyond softening the practice can be explained in the light of the EEA experience. It might reasonably be assumed that the "economic and regulatory integration" referred to by Stefano Micossi above as necessary to eliminate anti-dumping may have been in place in the case

---

21 For undertakings see Article 8 of basic anti-dumping Reg 384/96, OJ 1996 L56.
22 Council of the European Union (1994), Essen European Council, Conclusions of the Presidency, Annex IV.
23 See Sir Leon Brittan Seminar on Trade Defence Instruments, Brussels, 27 January 1997.
24 See *e.g.* Stanbrook & Bentley, *Dumping and Subsidies: The Law and Procedures Governing the Imposition of Anti-Dumping and Countervailing Duties in the European Community* (1996) Kluwer Law International, 179.

of the European Economic Area (EEA) Agreement between the EC and the EFTA countries. Within this the extension of the EC's four freedoms to the EFTA countries was accompanied by their adoption of much of the Community's *acquis*.

As such, the use of anti-dumping measures would have become unnecessary in the context of the competition rules and other regulatory alignment put into place. This was outlined in Article 26 of the EEA which states:

> "Anti-dumping measures, countervailing duties and measures against illicit commercial practices attributable to third countries shall not be applied in relations between the Contracting Parties, unless otherwise specified in this Agreement."

This latter point "unless otherwise specified in this Agreement" is clearly the significant one, leaving the door open to anti-dumping measures if necessary in areas where the *acquis communautaire* has not been fully extended to the EFTA countries. It is also significant that the major area where this provision removing the use of anti-dumping measures applied was in the fishery products sector. As Miranda points out, once the enlargement of the EU took place in 1995, fisheries was one of the most important sectors for two of the three remaining EFTA members.[25]

In contrast to Article 26 of the EEA proposing the removal of anti-dumping measures, Protocol 9 (Article 4.3) covering trade in fish merely states, in a phrase reminiscent of the position towards the associated countries of Central and Eastern Europe, that:

> "The Contracting Parties shall endeavour to ensure conditions of competition which will enable the other Contracting Parties to refrain from the application of anti-dumping measures and countervailing duties."

It is thus quite striking that in an agreement as extensive as the EEA in terms of the harmonisation of laws and regulations, such an important sector should be excluded from the removal of the anti-dumping instrument.

This exemption was brought into focus in 1996 when an anti-dumping case was initiated by the Community against farmed salmon coming from Norway. This followed complaints by the Community industry, primarily comprising Scottish salmon farmers that

---

25 J Miranda "Should anti-dumping laws be dumped?" (1996) *Law and Policy in International Business*, Vol 28(1) Fall issue,

Norwegian salmon at dumped prices was causing injury to the Community producers.

The case created much controversy and dissent within the EU including at the level of Commissioners when the DG I anti-dumping services attempted to introduce provisional anti-dumping measures. It was made more interesting by the fact that the complainants were largely from the United Kingdom, which as a Member State is traditionally an opponent of anti-dumping measures.

In addition, the fact that the case was against a member country of the EEA also raised certain concerns. Indeed, in a letter to Trade Commissioner, Sir Leon Brittan, the Swedish Government wrote that:

> "The EEA does not contain any formal obstacle to anti-dumping and countervailing action against salmon imports, but the spirit in our view calls on the union to try to solve trade issues through a dialogue, and avoid unilateral measures."[26]

It is this distinction between formal obstacles and the spirit of the agreement which is crucial here. It must not be forgotten in this instance though that Sweden is usually a firm opponent of anti-dumping measures anyway, and thus its interpretation of the "spirit" of the EEA may not be the interpretation of others. Certainly the fact that fisheries are explicitly excluded from the article proposing that anti-dumping should not be used suggests that this investigation was not necessarily such a surprise.

The deal which was finally negotiated in an effort to avoid anti-dumping duties resulted in a minimum price undertaking, a cap on the growth of salmon exports to the EU, an increase in Norway's own tax on salmon exporters and monitoring by the European Commission with duties automatically being imposed where the agreement is breached.[27]

From the point of view of competition and a levelling of the playing field the salmon case highlights the gaps in the EEA's rules and regulations which mean that the use of anti-dumping cannot be precluded. In contrast to the situation with other products, the broader and deeper legal harmonisation process within the overall *acquis communautaire* has not been sufficiently carried out in the fisheries sector and competition rules in themselves are not enough. Thus, instruments of trade defence remain.

---

26 Reported in *Financial Times*, 15 April 1997.
27 See *Financial Times*, 3 June 1997. Definitive Duties: Council Reg 1890/97, OJ 1997 L267.

Furthermore, this case is relevant in that the initial complaint was a twofold against, on one hand, dumping and, on the other, the granting of subsidies by the Norwegian Government. Consequently an anti-subsidy investigation was initiated alongside the anti-dumping one. This again illustrates the contrast between fisheries and other sectors since countervailing duties, like anti-dumping duties, are not allowed under Article 26 of the EEA other than in specifically named sectors.

The case of salmon is of wider interest from a trade and competition perspective since anti-dumping and competition investigations relating to Norwegian producers were conducted in this area in the early 1990s. A Community anti-dumping investigation was initiated against Norwegian salmon in February 1990 following complaints from Scottish and Irish producers. In March 1991, the Commission decided to close the case without imposing measures, however, on the grounds that prices had recovered and the measures were unnecessary. This was allied to action by the Norwegian government to restrict the volume of supply and curb surplus production. In June 1990, the Commission opened an investigation into an agreement between the Scottish salmon farmers and those in Norway regarding agreed minimum prices on the part of the Norwegians and appropriate price discipline from the Scottish producers.

Although the agreement was terminated at the end of 1991 the Commission Decision of July 1992 condemned the attempt to fix prices.[28] The Commission's competition Decision tried to establish a principle on the anti-dumping/competition interface by pointing out that undertakings, when faced with a situation of dumping, are not permitted "either in addition to or instead of an anti-dumping procedure, to enter into a restrictive private agreement in order to remedy the situation".[29]

## 3. Post-accession

### Previous enlargements

When Spain and Portugal joined the Community in 1986, the anti-dumping mechanism was retained for a short-period through a Council Regulation which allowed for anti-dumping measures between the new

---

28 Commission Dec of 30 July 1992, OJ 1992 L246.
29 See Commission of the European Communities: 22nd Annual Report on Competition Policy 1992, p102.

and the existing Member States and between the new Member States themselves during the transitional period of accession.[30] A similar arrangement had existed after the first enlargement of 1973 involving the United Kingdom, Ireland and Denmark although this was at a time before anti-dumping had become an important trade instrument and the arrangement was not called into action.

The policy adopted for the 1986 enlargement, however, was particularly interesting in the case of Spain which during the early 1980s, like the current applicants, had been quite a regular target of Community anti-dumping investigations. Indeed, between 1982 and 1985, the four years before accession, 17 investigations were initiated against Spanish products.

Where measures were already in force in either direction, these were reviewed by the Commission upon accession. New complaints could then be made to the Commission who would investigate in a similar manner to any other anti-dumping case. Significantly though it was DG IV, the Competition Directorate-General of the Commission, which took over responsibility for this rather than DG I (External Relations) which normally conducts anti-dumping investigations. The other notable difference was that decisions where made came in the form of recommendations to the firm in question that the dumping be terminated. Where this recommendation is not adhered to, or where undertakings are not offered or complied with, the Commission could apply anti-dumping duties. Therefore, in the case of choline chloride being exported from Belgium to Spain, following a complaint in 1987, the Commission, after consultation with the relevant Member State, issued a recommendation in 1988 proposing a minimum price to the Belgian producer which the producer undertook to accept.[31] It is interesting to note that the dumping in this case was being carried out by a producer in an established rather than a new Member State.

This provision which expired at the end of 1992 was little used, and most of the measures in force before accession were repealed, but it provides an interesting example of how the Community incorporated new Member States into its anti-dumping regime. When the 1995 enlargement took place to include Sweden, Finland and Austria (all of whom were already in the EEA Agreement) the Community's anti-dumping legislation took immediate effect.

---

30 Council Reg 812/86, OJ 1986 L78.
31 See Commission of the European Communities: 18th Annual Report on Competition Policy 1988.

The experience of Spain and Portugal, although one might think a better example for the Central and East European countries than the EEA countries, may not in fact be so. Stefano Micossi, for example, points out that the maintenance of the anti-dumping instrument in the case of the 1986 enlargement corresponded to a period in which trade barriers were being progressively removed. He contrasts this with the CEECs whereby all tariff barriers are due to be removed by 2001, and the Europe Agreements and Accession Strategy provide a momentum for integration if not an environment exactly comparable to the EEA. It is clear that the gradual phasing out of the anti-dumping instrument which should ensue as the *acquis* is taken on board in the applicant countries should remove the need for the kind of transitional period seen in 1986.

## Eastern enlargement

In the next enlargement, when the associated countries join the EU, the situation will change to one where the EU's competition rules become the dominant instrument to ensure "fairness", there having, in the meantime, been a general regulatory harmonisation.

Practices which may have fallen foul of the Community's anti-dumping rules will, if anywhere, be dealt with by the competition rules (Article 86) post-accession, and possibly state aids rules.[32] In practice, however, the fact that anti-dumping and competition rules nowadays are not addressing the same problems means that this is not likely to be an issue for the Central and East European producers.

Perhaps more relevant will be the fact that these countries will, post-accession, become "insiders" in the EU's anti-dumping process and thus their imports could potentially be subject to anti-dumping measures. As such, they will also be involved in making the decisions on whether to impose EU-wide duties through their position on the Anti-Dumping Advisory Committee and in the Council of Ministers. Their domestic producers will be able to make complaints against non-EU imports which may result in anti-dumping measures, assuming that the necessary criteria are met. In addition, of course, Central and East European importers, users and customers may be faced with higher prices where their imports from third countries are subject to existing or new anti-dumping measures. As such these countries will have to

---

32 Anti-dumping in practice is often used as a surrogate for countervailing duties.

weigh up the interests of their producer and user industries when making the decision to impose or not to impose measures.

This has taken on an added salience in Poland with the 1997 adoption of their own anti-dumping legislation. The regulation is largely, but not entirely, based on that of the EU and the degree to which it is used in the years up to accession could prove very interesting. Anti-dumping laws are also now in place in Bulgaria, Czech Republic, Romania, Slovak Republic and Slovenia.

## 4. Conclusion

The proposed eastward enlargement of the EU is unusual in that the Europe Agreement countries are being asked to adopt the whole internal market *acquis* before they are given unconditional access to the EU market and before the institutional framework of membership is in place.

We can usefully contrast the treatment of countries with Europe Agreements with that of the European Economic Area with respect to anti-dumping. The EEA states are exempted from anti-dumping action for all sectors of the economy unless the sector concerned is explicitly excluded by reason of not applying the *acquis communautaire*. The Europe Association partners are fully subject to commercial policy instruments but the application of these could be "progressively reduced" as the acquis are applied. This provides us with a possible answer to the question: how can, say, a Polish firm ensure that what it does is not going to make it subject it to anti-dumping?[33]

The problem could be resolved if, in the course of the recently announced Accession Partnerships, the EU and partner countries could agree a stamp of approval for sectors where the acquis were deemed to have been fully complied with, or at least as fully as is the case within Member States. Where there is an open market and no private barriers to entry, and an absence of upstream or downstream distortions capable of giving rise to accusations of a non–level playing field, such sectors could be deemed to be dumping-free zones. We have argued that the EU is unlikely to give unconditional guarantees of anti-dumping free access until the internal market *acquis* are at least as definitely entrenched as in the EEA. But even if a legally binding renunciation of

33 NB Where constructed values are possible, the charging of identical prices at home and abroad can still lead to charges of dumping if it is claimed that there are distortions in the background which lead to the home prices not being true normal values.

the anti-dumping weapon may be too much to hope for, there is a good chance that the Commission and Council could promise not to impose anti-dumping duties on any goods from industries which had received the kind of "certification" we have spoken of. This would provide a clear incentive to the CEEC partners to adopt the *acquis* and also might sharpen Commission's collective mind on just what a "level' playing field means.[34]

In the absence of such a sector–by–sector approach, the implication of Community policy is that as the Europe Agreements are progressively applied anti-dumping should fade away as a practical policy instrument in the run up to enlargement, but it will remain as a weapon of last resort until actual accession takes place. In practice the EU producers may also be less likely to make the expensive and time-consuming complaints necessary to open an investigation if it appears that the relief will end on accession and thus only be short-lived. By this time, if all has gone well, the need for transitional post-accession anti-dumping arrangements as per the Spanish experience should have disappeared and the candidate countries will find themselves transformed very quickly from anti-dumping poachers to game keepers (or should it be the other way round?).

Jeremy Kempton
Dr Peter Holmes

---

34 It remains to be seen whether this could provide enough of an incentive for countries not in the first wave of negotiations.

# · Index ·